Discover Eltham and

Discover
ELTHAM
and its ENVIRONS

A comprehensive guide to ELTHAM,
ELTHAM PALACE, NEW ELTHAM, MOTTINGHAM,
KIDBROOKE, & SHOOTERS HILL

by DARRELL SPURGEON

GREENWICH GUIDE-BOOKS

Copyright © Darrell Spurgeon 2000

All rights reserved. No part of this book may be copied or otherwise reproduced, stored in a retrieval system, or transmitted, in any form or by any means, electronic, mechanical, photocopying, recording or otherwise, without the prior permission of the author.

First published in Great Britain 1992 by
Greenwich Guide-Books,
72 Kidbrooke Grove, Blackheath, London SE 3
(phone 020-8858 5831)
Second edition, extensively revised, 2000

Other volumes in the same series by the same author:
Volume I (first edition), covering Woolwich, Plumstead, Shooters Hill, East Wickham, Abbey Wood & Thamesmead (published 1990, out of print)
Volume II, covering Greenwich, Westcombe & Charlton (published 1991, out of print)
Volume III, covering Eltham, New Eltham, Mottingham, Grove Park, Kidbrooke & Shooters Hill (published 1992, out of print)
Volume IV, covering Bexley, Bexleyheath, Welling, Sidcup, Footscray & North Cray (published 1993)
Volume V, covering Crayford, Slade Green, Erith, Belvedere, Abbey Wood & Thamesmead (published 1995)
Volume VI (new edition of Volume I), covering Woolwich, The Royal Arsenal, Woolwich Common, Plumstead, Shooters Hill & Abbey Wood (published 1996)
Volume VII, covering Deptford, New Cross, Brockley, Lewisham & Ladywell (published 1997, out of print)
Volume VIII, covering Sydenham, Crystal Palace, Forest Hill, Catford, Hither Green & Grove Park (published 1999)

Front cover photograph is Great Hall, Eltham Palace (late 1470s) - *gazetteer reference Eltham 1*

Printed in the UK by The Hackney Press

A catalogue record for this book is available from the British Library
ISBN 0 9515624 8 7

CONTENTS

Foreword   page 7

ELTHAM
Introduction   11
Gazetteer - Section 'A' (Eltham Palace)   15
Gazetteer - Section 'B' (Crown Lands)   21
Gazetteer - Section 'C' (High Street & Southend)   29
Gazetteer - Section 'D' (Avery Hill)   37
Gazetteer - Section 'E' (Eltham Park)   43
Gazetteer - Section 'F' (Well Hall)   47
Suggested Walks   51

NEW ELTHAM
Gazetteer   55
Suggested Walk   58

MOTTINGHAM
Introduction   59
Gazetteer   61
Suggested Walk   67

KIDBROOKE
Introduction   68
Gazetteer   71
Suggested Walk   77

SHOOTERS HILL
Introduction   78
Gazetteer   81
Suggested Walk   87

Notes on some architects & artists   89
Bibliography   92
Index   94

MAPS
Eltham & its Environs   6
General Map of Eltham   10
  Map of Sections 'A' & 'B' (Eltham Palace & Crown Lands)   22
  Map of Section 'C' (High Street & Southend)   30
  Map of Section 'D' (Avery Hill)   38
  Map of Section 'E' (Eltham Park)   42
  Map of Section 'F' (Well Hall)   48
Map of New Eltham   56
Map of Mottingham   62
Map of Kidbrooke   70
Map of Shooters Hill   80

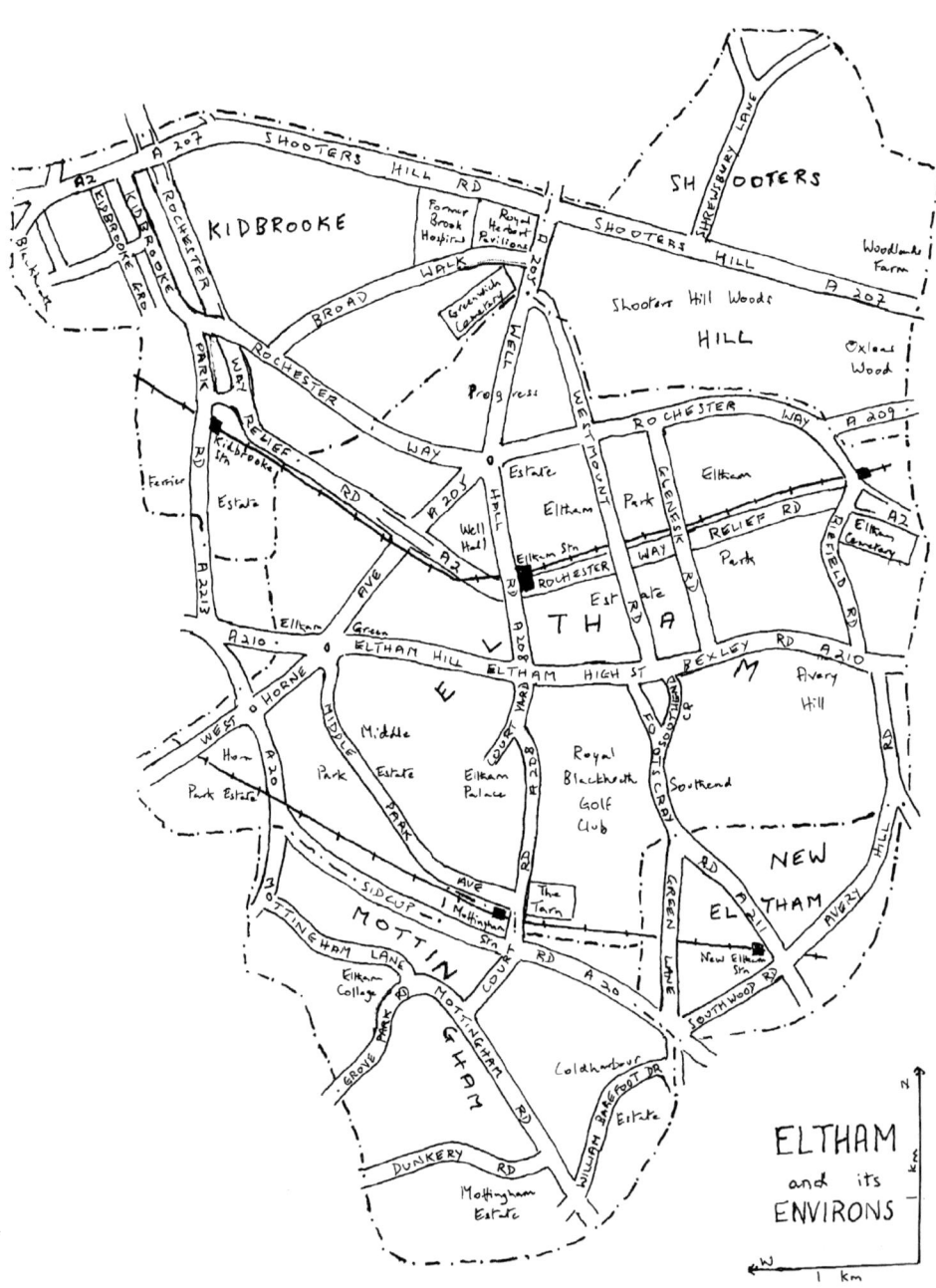

FOREWORD

The first edition of this book appeared in 1992, and has been out of print for several years. This new edition has been extensively revised and rewritten. The section on Eltham Palace has been updated and takes into account the new public access to Courtauld House. Many new locations in Eltham have been included, and some new locations in New Eltham and the other areas as well.

To make way, as it were, for the additional text in a book of this size, the area of Grove Park has been omitted in this new edition. However, a revised description of this area was included in the previous book in the series, 'Discover Sydenham and Catford', published in 1999. In addition, the description of Morden College which was included (improperly) under Kidbrooke in the first edition has been omitted.

This book covers five areas- Eltham, New Eltham, Mottingham, Kidbrooke, and Shooters Hill. The boundaries between the areas, which are topographical (rather than administrative) boundaries, are shown on the map opposite. People living in some areas covered by this book may be surprised to find their area described as within the environs of Eltham. New Eltham and Mottingham are clearly within the environs; so are the eastern parts of Kidbrooke and the southern half of Shooters Hill, and it would not seem logical to exclude the remainder of these two areas. As in the previous book, the boundary of Kidbrooke has been extended to the west to include an area which would nowadays be considered to be part of Blackheath (though it was in fact mostly part of the old parish of Kidbrooke).

This volume overlaps with the section on Shooters Hill in a book in this series published in 1996, the revised edition of 'Discover Woolwich and its Environs'; it is hoped this will not be considered an unnecessary duplication, in fact the entry on Woodlands Farm has been updated and considerably enlarged.

Eltham, New Eltham, Kidbrooke and Shooters Hill are in the London Borough of Greenwich; from 1900 to 1965 they were part of the Metropolitan Borough of Woolwich, except for Kidbrooke, which was part of the Metropolitan Borough of Greenwich. Mottingham is partly in the London Borough of Greenwich and partly in the London Borough of Bromley, with the boundary running roughly along the line of Mottingham Road and the Little Quaggy River.

For each area there is a basic framework consisting of brief introduction, gazetteer, map(s) and suggested walk(s). The introduction to Eltham also covers New Eltham, to which there is no separate introduction. Each area has one or more maps and a detailed gazetteer. Every location in the gazetteer is identified (using location numbers) on a map. There are also suggested walks, but only where places of interest are concentrated within an area which makes walking practicable and interesting, and where guidance would be helpful.

8 - FOREWORD

Eltham is divided into six sections - Section 'A' - Eltham Palace; Section 'B' - Crown Lands; Section 'C' - High Street & Southend; Section 'D' - Avery Hill; Section 'E' - Eltham Park; and Section 'F' - Well Hall - and has five maps (one covering two sections). The boundary between the sections is shown on the general map on page 10. There are suggested walks covering most locations in each section.

The other four areas - New Eltham, Mottingham, Kidbrooke and Shooters Hill - are not divided into sections. Each area has a map. Suggested walks cover all locations in New Eltham, and most locations in Mottingham and Shooters Hill, but the western part only of Kidbrooke (otherwise the walk would be too long).

Although the introductions to the areas contain some historical background, and certain locations have some historical information in indented paragraphs, the guide is not a history of Eltham and the surrounding areas; it makes no pretensions to be a work of local history. Again, although some non-specialist knowledge of architecture is assumed, the guide does not become involved in detailed architectural analysis, and a conscious attempt has been made to avoid architectural jargon. Readers interested in further information on local history and architectural detail may like to consult the list of books at the end of the guide.

The gazetteers are intended as a comprehensive list of buildings and landscape features which are of visual interest, though the choice of places is inevitably very personal. The emphasis is on what is there now, not so much on what has been there in the past, and practical information is given on how best to see each place. The starring system in the gazetteers, with stars being given to the most outstanding locations, is intended to help visitors to allocate their time to the best advantage.

The maps, which are the key to the guide, adopt the same practical approach. Nearly every place mentioned in the text is pinpointed on a map in such a way as to make it easy to find and notice. The maps are indicative and not to scale, and only show those roads which are likely to be important to the visitor. It is suggested that a proper and more detailed road map of the area also be obtained.

When using the gazetteers and following the suggested walks, it is advisable always to try to have a clear idea of the direction you are facing, ie north, south, east or west.

Italics are used for information on access, for other practical advice, for introductory notes before the walks, and also for cross-referencing. Paragraphs with information of a specifically historical nature are indented.

The sequence of locations in the gazetteers broadly follows the order in the suggested walks, and locations not included in the walks are slotted into the sequence in a way which would make it more convenient for a visit.

Some locations are difficult of access, and the guide gives practical information on how to overcome this difficulty. In some cases this may not always be possible, but it is certainly worth trying. In other cases, a certain initiative is demanded; for example, it is usually necessary to phone or call at the clergyman's residence to obtain access to church interiors. In my experience most clergymen are extremely helpful in facilitating this. And many places which are private will not in practice turn away the interested visitor asking permission to view. The text includes contact telephone numbers and/or addresses which may be found helpful in this context.

Of the publications which I have consulted, I wish to make particular mention of: 'London 2: South', by Bridget Cherry and Nikolaus Pevsner, in the Penguin Buildings of England series; the Department of the Environment List of Buildings of Architectural & Historic Interest, which can be consulted at the National Monuments Record (London office), 55 Blandford Street, London W1; the Local List of Buildings published and updated by the Planning Department of the London Borough of Greenwich, which is available in local libraries; the official guide to Eltham Palace, by Michael Turner; 'Eltham, a Pictorial History', by John Kennett; 'Kidbrooke', by Michael Egan; 'Blackheath Village and Environs, Volume Two', by the Blackheath local historian Neil Rhind, which covers part of the area of Kidbrooke; and 'Eltham in the Making', and other informative publications of The Eltham Society. My debt to these publications is enormous. Other books which I have found useful are included in the bibliography at the end.

I also wish to give very special thanks and acknowledgment to numerous local people who helped me in various ways in preparing this new edition.

In particular, John Kennett, the Eltham historian, read an initial draft of the whole text. He made many constructive criticisms, provided much factual information, stopped me going astray in numerous ways, and suggested a number of important leads for me to follow. The final text is enriched by his contribution. Julian Watson, of the Local History Library of the London Borough of Greenwich at Woodlands, Mycenae Road, Blackheath, also read the whole text, and made many helpful comments. Dr John Priestley, of Edinburgh, read the text on Eltham Palace and gave a lot of factual advice; the publication of his history of the Palace is eagerly awaited. Wynn Parkinson read the text on Mottingham, and made many helpful comments; the revised edition of her booklet on Mottingham is also eagerly awaited.

Julian Watson and the supporting staff of the Greenwich Local History Library at Woodlands - Frances Ward, Jennie O'Keeffe and Caroline Warhurst - dealt courteously and efficiently with my many requests for information. Many thanks also to Tony Dunlop, Secretary of the Royal Blackheath Golf Club; Anthea Gent, for showing me around Holy Trinity Church; Sister Catherine, of the Convent of Mercy; Dave Vaughan, for taking me on a walk around Woodlands Farm; the staff at the British Architectural Library, of the Royal Institute of British Architects. Clergymen at all the churches were helpful in facilitating my visits, but I wish to make a very special mention of Rev Wendy Saunders, the vicar of St Saviour, Middle Park, who provided a lot of information and offered good advice on the several visits I made to the church.

The area covered by this guide, like any urban area, is subject to the process of change, and the situation with regard to the condition and function (or even the existence) of buildings, their accessibility etc can change quite rapidly. However, the information was checked before going to print, and if anyone is misled in any way, I can only offer my apologies.

Darrell Spurgeon,

Blackheath, July 2000

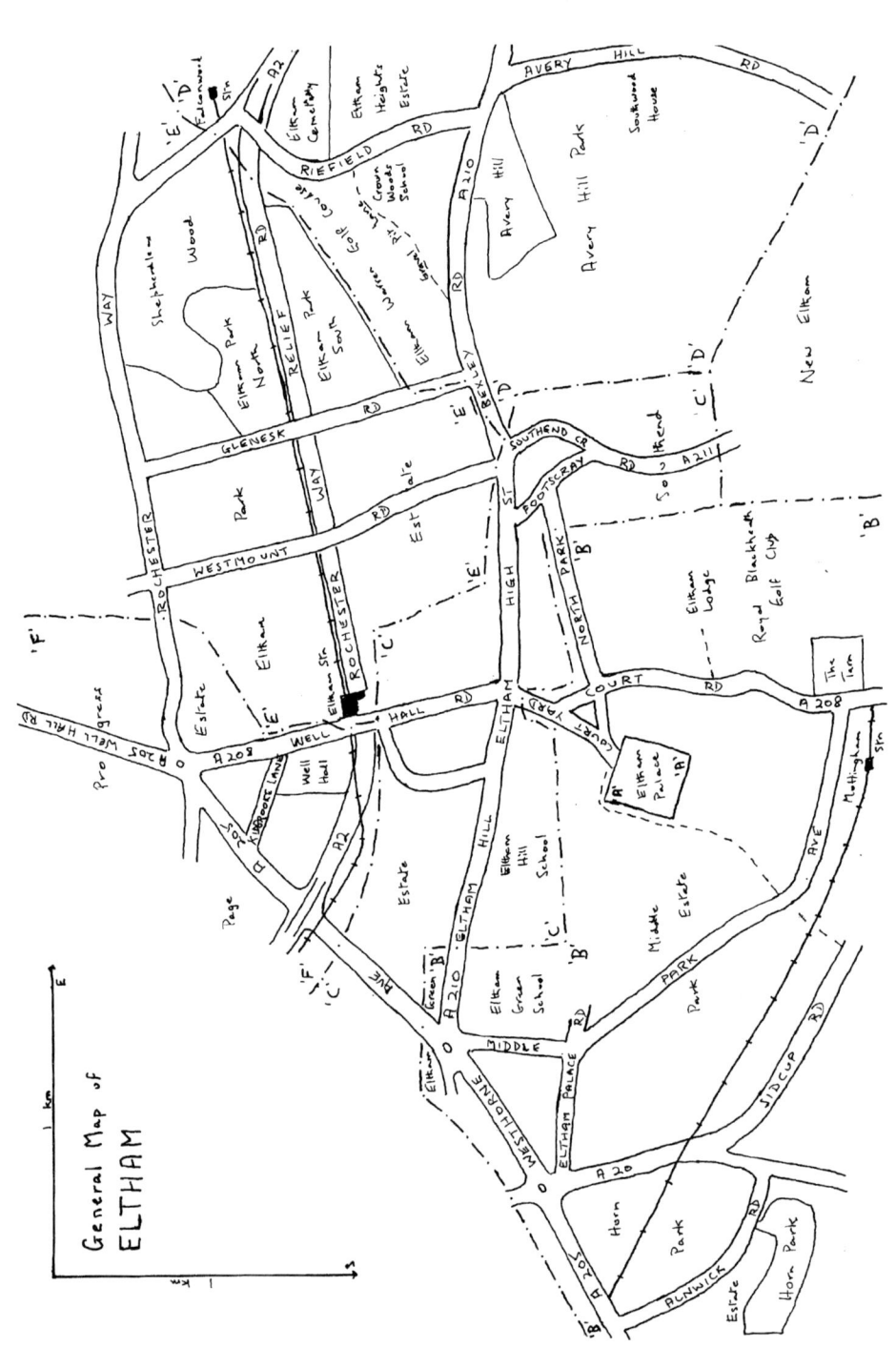

ELTHAM

Introduction

Eltham is a historical town enveloped by the growth of the London conurbation. It contains two sites of outstanding importance, both linked with its history as the home of a royal palace, and there are many other important buildings and interesting areas.

The moated site of Eltham Palace is one of the most evocative relics of a medieval royal palace in the country. The Great Hall, the moat bridge and some moat walling have survived from the medieval period, and the Lord Chancellor's Lodgings is the main survivor from the Tudor period.

Eltham Lodge was built in the former royal Great Park in the 17th century. Designed by Hugh May, it was one of the earliest, and one of the finest, domestic mansions in the new classical style in the London area.

Eltham is surrounded by great areas of open space which prevent its submergence in suburbia. To the west are the sports grounds and old farmlands around the Quaggy River, to the south the former Great Park and the fields around King John's Walk, to the east the parklands of Eltham Park and Avery Hill, and to the north the Shooters Hill Woods.

Early history

Roman remains have been found at Archery Road and at Glenesk Road, and the finds are in the Borough Museum, at present located at Plumstead.

But Eltham's recorded history begins with a mention in the Domesday Book of 1086, by which time the area was relatively quite populous. Its strategic situation on a ridge, overhanging the land watered by the Quaggy River and dominating the south-eastern approaches to London, led to the establishment c1300 of a moated manor house, which soon became a royal palace.

Eltham Palace

Eltham Palace was one of the principal royal palaces on the outskirts of London for 200 years. The royal manor of Eltham during that period stretched from Shooters Hill in the north to Mottingham and Coldharbour in the south, and from Lee in the west to Southend in the east.

But by the 1530s Henry VIII had begun to show a preference for Greenwich Palace, and during the reign of Elizabeth I Eltham went into decline, though the vast parklands - Great Park, Middle Park and Horn Park - were used for hunting.

Tudor Eltham

During the Tudor period Eltham consisted mainly of the royal palace and grounds, the village around the old parish church, and a kilometre to the north, the separate estate of Well Hall (which dates back at least to the 13th century). A Tudor mansion at Well Hall was occupied by William Roper, who married Sir Thomas More's daughter Margaret in 1521; an outlying building, called the Tudor Barn, has survived and is now a pub.

The Tudor period also saw the beginning of the small hamlets of Southend to the east, and Pope Street to the south. Pope Street, along what is now Avery Hill Road, was to develop into the railway suburb of New Eltham.

The church and the High Street

There has been a church on the site of St Johns Church since at least c1160, though the present church dates from 1875.

Eltham Village developed on both sides of the church along the route of the present High Street, and in Court Yard, which linked the High Street with the Palace. By the early 18th century the High Street was largely built-up, with several larger houses. Two of these houses, of c1720, have survived - Cliefden and Queenscroft. Other survivors from that time are the Orangery, dilapidated but elegant, from the garden of the now demolished Eltham House; the Greyhound pub; and its neighbour Mellins, now a wine bar.

In the 1780s the New Cross Turnpike Trust improved the old track which ran up Eltham Hill and along the High Street, then turned south via the present Southend Crescent and Footscray Road. It was part of the route from London Bridge to Footscray, and three of the original milestones have survived.

The village was originally more cohesive than it is today, for there was no major crossroads by the church. The road to Well Hall followed the curving route of the present Sherard Road; that part of Well Hall Road which exists now to the south of the railway was not constructed until 1905.

The High Street retained a strong village atmosphere until the rebuilding and road-widening of the interwar period. Even now it has a special character, perhaps best exemplified by the grouping of Mellins and The Greyhound; and by lanes like Philipot Path and Orangery Lane which, although bleak in parts, are recognisably old village lanes.

Great houses

Eltham Palace was, apart from the Great Hall, largely destroyed during the Civil War. The vast parklands were leased by Charles II to his former banker Sir John Shaw, who in 1664 built Eltham Lodge in the new classical style in the middle of Great Park. Eltham Lodge is now the clubhouse of the Royal Blackheath Golf Club.

The Tudor moated mansion of Well Hall was demolished by the developer Sir Gregory Page when he acquired the Roper Estate in 1733, though a substantial building outside the moat, now called the Tudor Barn, has survived. Page built a new house, also called Well Hall, to the east of the moat; this house was occupied from 1899 to 1922 by the writer Edith Nesbit and her husband Hubert Bland, a founder of the Fabian Society. The house was damaged by fire in 1926 and subsequently demolished.

Park Farm Place was built by the naval commander Sir William James in 1774 on the site of an earlier 18th century mansion; the lands were vast, covering the area of the Eltham Park Estate and Eltham Park, and extending to Shooters Hill Woods. Severndroog Castle was built just north of the grounds by his widow to commemorate him in 1784. The mansion was subsequently called Eltham Park House, and St Mary's School, Glenure Road, is now on the site. The estate was sold to the developer Cameron Corbett in 1900.

An extraordinary phenomenon was the building in 1890 of an enormous and ostentatious mansion on the estate of Avery Hill to the east of the High Street by the 'nitrate king' John North. It is now part of the University of Greenwich, and the grounds include a public park. Within the grounds is the late 18th century Southwood House, in an area once known as Polecat End.

Sir Stephen Courtauld built Eltham Hall in 1936 adjoining the Great Hall of Eltham Palace. The house, an outstanding example of art deco style, is now called Courtauld House; it is managed by English Heritage, and together with the Great Hall and the moat and gardens of the Palace, is the most important visitor attraction of Eltham.

The arrival of the railway

Mottingham Station was the first station in the Eltham area; it was opened on the Dartford Loop Line in 1866, and was then called Eltham Station. It was sited so far south in order to avoid crossing the grounds of Eltham Lodge. At that time there was virtually no housing between Eltham High Street and Court Yard in the north and Mottingham Lane in the south.

Court Road was constructed shortly after the opening of the station along the line of an old farm track, and the large houses along its west side began to appear from 1869. Other housing developments in this period took place in the northern part of Court Yard and in Wythfield Road; and some distance away, in the eastern part of North Park and the northern part of Footscray Road. Housing along the east side of Court Road did not develop until the early 1890s.

New Eltham Station, further down the Loop Line, was the next to be opened, in 1878. The station was then called Pope Street, the name of the old hamlet along Avery Hill Road. At that time the area was sparsely inhabited; the only pre-railway buildings which survive are Theobalds Cottages and The Grange.

With the coming of the railway New Eltham began to develop quite rapidly. A number of large houses were built, along Southwood Road, in Merchland Road and Eastnor Road, and in nearby parts of Avery Hill Road and Footscray Road. Smaller terraced houses were built in roads opposite the station, and along Footscray Road to the north of The Beehive pub.

Early housing estates

Housing in the central area of Eltham did not develop on any scale until after the opening of Well Hall Station, the first centrally located station, on the Bexleyheath Line in 1895.

The Eltham Park Estate of Cameron Corbett was started in 1900, and was well under way when Eltham Park Station was opened specifically for the estate in 1908. (With the construction of the Rochester Way Relief Road both these stations have now been closed and merged into the new Eltham Station.)

The Corbett Estate was followed by an estate, with graceful rows of bow-fronted houses, built from 1906 to 1912 in the angle between Well Hall Road and Sherard Road.

The extraordinary Well Hall Estate was built in 1915 for workers at the Royal Arsenal at Woolwich; it was renamed Progress Estate when purchased by the Royal Arsenal Co-operative Society in 1925. Also built for Arsenal workers in 1916 were settlements of huts which almost encircled the Well Hall Estate; these were all replaced between the wars.

Suburban growth

At the end of the first world war Eltham still remained largely agricultural, with housing development largely confined to the north of the area, but this was to change in the interwar period.

New major roads began to set natural boundaries to the area on all sides except the east - Sidcup Road in 1923, Rochester Way in 1930, and Westhorne Avenue in the early 1930s. The High Street was widened in the 1920s, and by the outbreak of war had begun to foreshadow today's shopping centre.

Several large cottage-style housing estates were built by the then Metropolitan Borough of Woolwich to cover farmland to the south and west of Eltham. The large Page Estate, stretching from Eltham Hill north to Rochester Way, was developed through the 1920s on land acquired by Sir Gregory Page in 1733 from the Roper Estate. The Middle Park and Horn Park Estates, both with many mock-Tudor houses, were built in the old palace parklands in the 1930s.

The so-called Eltham Heights Estate was a private development on the former Avery Hill Farm from 1934, planned with a spacious layout along picturesque winding streets, and with a delightful green on Fairoak Drive.

New housing estates were built around New Eltham, and this area had become built up, with a small shopping centre, by the 1930s.

Postwar

The only major postwar housing development in Eltham has been the Avery Hill Estate, built by the London County Council to the east of Avery Hill Park. However, the larger Coldharbour Estate was built on Coldharbour Farm in the eastern part of Mottingham.

Eltham had already seemed to be overwhelmed by major roads, and this was accentuated by the construction in 1988 of the motorway-type Rochester Way Relief Road. It parallels the railway as it slices through the heart of the area, approaching from the west on an embankment, then descending under the forecourt of the new Eltham Station into a cutting through the Corbett Estate and Eltham Park.

# ELTHAM

Gazetteer

Section 'A' ELTHAM PALACE

1. *****Eltham Palace** was an important royal palace from medieval to Tudor times. Most of the palace buildings have disappeared, but the remains are of outstanding interest and appeal. Within the moated area of the palace, they consist of the **Great Hall** with its screens passage, the bridge and moat walls, some excavated areas, and some minor structures. A large part of the site is still surrounded by a moat.

Alongside the medieval Great Hall is **Courtauld House**, built for Sir Stephen and Lady Virginia Courtauld 1934-36; the exterior is in a restrained classical style, but the interior is an outstanding example of art deco. It was the Headquarters of the Royal Army Educational Corps from 1945 to 1992.

English Heritage, after assuming full responsibility for the moated site and gardens in 1995, undertook a comprehensive restoration. They set out to recreate the lavishly furnished interior of Courtauld House as it was in the late 1930s. This major initiative was completed and opened to the public in 1999; it is a wonderful place to visit.

> The Palace, Courtauld House and the grounds are open to the public on Wednesdays, Thursdays, Fridays and Sundays only, 1000-1800 April to September, 1000-1700 October, 1000-1600 November to March. Telephone 020 8294 2548. It is not possible to visit the Great Hall without passing through Courtauld House. Admission charge (including an audio tour); free to members of English Heritage. Access is from Court Yard by the bridge across the north moat. The car park is reached by an entrance off Court Road.
> When the Palace is closed, the moat bridge, the north moat wall, the north wall of the Great Hall and the front of Courtauld House can be viewed from the end of Court Yard.

Eltham Palace was first built c1300 as a manor house by Bishop Anthony Bek of Durham; it had a stone retaining wall, and was surrounded by a moat. In 1305 he presented it to the Prince of Wales, later Edward II. Bishop Bek continued living there until his death in 1311.

Edward II granted the manor to his queen Isabella, who constructed a new stronger stone moat wall with buttresses, large parts of which still survive. In 1344 the Palace passed to their son Edward III, who extended the buildings considerably in the 1350s.

Prince John of Eltham, the second son of Edward II and Isabella, was born at Eltham Palace in 1316, and spent much of his short life there; he acted as Regent of England when his elder brother Edward III was in France. He died of a fever in 1336; a striking effigy and tomb to Prince John (though now without its canopy) are in St Edmund's Chapel, Westminster Abbey; annually in October flowers from the Palace are laid there by Eltham schoolchildren (under the sponsorship of The Eltham Society).

Eltham became one of the principal royal palaces on the outskirts of London for the next 200 years. Royal apartments were built on the west side of the moated site for the first time during the reign of Henry IV, and substantial alterations and extensions were carried out during subsequent reigns. The present Great Hall and the moat bridge were probably built by Edward IV in the late 1470s. The excavated footings of the royal apartments, which are now visible, belong to rebuilding from the 1520s to c1604.

Distinguished visitors included King Jean le Bon of France, who during his years of voluntary exile after defeat at Poitiers in 1356 stayed at the Palace in 1360 and 1364. Geoffrey Chaucer, who was Clerk of Works for the royal palaces 1389-91, probably stayed there; on two occasions, on his way from Westminster to Eltham, he was robbed at Hatcham (near New Cross). Jean Froissart, the French chronicler, was there in 1364 and again in 1396. The Byzantine Emperor, Manuel Palaeologus, spent Christmas there with Henry IV in 1400. Henry V entered into an alliance with the Holy Roman Emperor, Sigismund, there in 1416.

(At times the Palace has been popularly known as King John's Court or King John's Palace. An adjoining lane is still called King John's Walk, *see 5*. There is no definite explanation for this. It probably refers to King Jean le Bon of France, but it may derive from Prince John of Eltham.)

Henry VIII was born at the Palace of Placentia at Greenwich. During the early part of his reign he spent much time at Eltham, but by the 1530s his preferred palace in the area was Greenwich. In 1528 Henry VIII built a new chapel, whose foundations have been excavated (though they are now hidden beneath the north lawn).

At the end of the 16th century the palace consisted of the Great Court, containing the royal apartments, chapel and Great Hall, separated by a moat from the Green Court (of which only the Lord Chancellor's Lodgings survive); beyond the Green Court was the Outer Courtyard and the Tiltyard.

During the reign of Elizabeth I the palace had begun to decline in importance. However, the vast royal parklands - Great Park to the east, Middle Park to the south, and Horn Park to the west - continued in use for royal hunting parties up to the reign of Charles I.

The palace was (apart from the Great Hall) largely destroyed during the period of the Commonwealth. In 1663 Sir John Shaw, who had financed Charles II during that period, obtained a share of the lease of the Palace grounds. In 1664 Shaw built Eltham Lodge in the new classical style in the middle of Great Park (it is now the clubhouse of the Royal Blackheath Golf Club.) The palace site became part of Court Farm, the Great Hall was used as a barn, and the parklands became farmland. This continued until the early 19th century, when private houses began to appear within the moated site and the farm moved away.

In 1912-14 the government undertook major repairs of the Great Hall. In 1933 Sir Stephen Courtauld obtained the lease of the Great Court, and the restoration of the Hall was then completed, with some modern additions. Courtauld also demolished the more recent houses and built Eltham Hall, now known as Courtauld House, alongside the Great Hall. He extended the moat (by then confined to the north side) along the east and part of the west sides, laid it out with fountains and islands, and surrounded it with gardens.

After the war the Courtaulds did not wish to return to Eltham; in 1945 they transferred the remainder of the lease to the Royal Army Educational Corps, which remained at Eltham until 1992. English Heritage, which had assumed responsibility for the Great Hall in 1984, assumed control of the entire site in 1995; it was opened to the public in 1999. The site, still in the ownership of the Crown, continues to be managed by English Heritage.

English Heritage have published an excellent souvenir guidebook by Michael Turner, which is available on entering the Palace. It provides much fuller information on the history of the Palace and on the Courtauld family than the brief notes above, as well as much more detail on what to see during a visit than the following account, which is only intended as a summary. Visitors to the Palace are strongly recommended to obtain the English Heritage official guide.

The sequence of the route described here is: the exterior of the buildings, viewed from the north side; the interior of both Courtauld House and the Great Hall; the garden front of the buildings; the moat and gardens.

Approach to the site is over the moat bridge - by foot from Court Yard, or by a path from the car park. In the car park, the red brick wall to the north is a Tudor wall which probably separated the tiltyard from the Palace orchard. Around are greenhouses and sheds of the late 1930s. On the way to the entrance you pass a rose garden, and a further stretch of the Tudor red brick wall.

The **moat bridge**, which is stone-faced and has four Gothic arches, probably dates from the late 1470s. The brick parapet is probably c1828, the stone coping being salvaged from repairs to the Great Hall at that time. From the bridge there is a wonderful view of the moat, and of the north range of the **moat wall**, which is mainly stone of the early 14th century in the lower parts and brick of the Tudor period above; note the large irregular bastion at the north-west corner, and the smaller projecting bastion at the north-east corner. Just east of the bridge a lion and unicorn from the Houses of Parliament were incorporated into the wall in the 1930s, flanking a medieval window moved from elsewhere in the Palace.

Immediately to the left on crossing the bridge is a fragment of the Tudor gatehouse, with a tiny rounded opening. Then, from the front or north lawn, Courtauld House is to the left, the Great Hall straight ahead, and the excavations area to the right. The ticket office is to the left.

*Courtauld House** (originally called **Eltham Hall**) was built adjoining the Great Hall for Sir Stephen and Lady Virginia Courtauld by John Seely (later Lord Mottistone) and Paul Paget 1934-36. It consists of two wings at a strange butterfly angle (one wing adjoining the Great Hall), linked by a one storey entrance hall. This angle enabled the preservation in public view of three half-timbered Tudor gables from the Palace; situated along the roofline above the entrance, they are best seen through a window within the building, but on the exterior they become visible as one steps back some distance from the entrance.

The exterior of Courtauld House is both romantic and classical. The three towers or pavilions have French chateau style copper roofs, topped by small chesspiece figures. A Tudor-style section and the projecting spiral staircase on the right were designed to ease the transition from the main building to the Great Hall. The entrance is in a curved arcade with Ionic columns; above the door is a sculpture by Carlton Attwood representing Hospitality.

To the right is the north side of the **Great Hall**, built by Edward IV in the late 1470s. The exterior, stone-faced with Reigate ashlar, has a high-placed series of windows, and a fine bay at the west end with double rows of windows. Note the grotesque heads, the small Tudor window beyond the west bay, and Edward IV's emblem 'rose en soleil' in the spandrels above the entrance archway.

The original brick facing of the Great Hall can be seen on the west wall above the single storey extension, which was a squash court added in 1936. At the west end of the extension is a bronze statue of St George as Jason, by Alfred Hardiman 1930.

Along the west side of the Great Court, by the moat wall, is the *excavations area**, where foundations of the west front of the royal apartments were excavated in the 1950s. These apartments were, until they were destroyed during the Commonwealth, as high as the Great Hall. However, a wire barrier inhibits a close look.

Basically, to the left are footings of the king's apartments, built by Henry VIII in the 1520s and refronted by Elizabeth I in the 1580s, and to the right footings of the queen's apartments, built by James I c1604. Some of the stone foundations which have also been exposed are older, and may date back to the 14th century. A corridor between bay windows of the apartments and the moat wall is in places clearly visible.

Further to the right, the marble well-head on the lawn is 18th century Italian, imported in the late 1930s; the well itself is much older. From near this point there are good views over South London. Beyond are remains of a medieval long gallery, the inner wall of stone and the outer wall of brick. This leads to remains of three sides of an octagonal corner turret, erected by Bishop Bek c1300.

At the end is the upper part of the Tudor north moat wall, stretching as far as the bridge; it is of brick, with tiny round-headed openings.

(In 1976/8 an undercroft and a section of tiled pavement from the original manor house c1300, as well as the foundations of Henry VIII's chapel were excavated, but these are now hidden beneath the lawn. The excavations also found traces of 11th century buildings, as well as Roman rooftiles and Saxon pottery.)

The ***interior** of **Courtauld House** is quite extraordinary, mainly in art deco style, often reminiscent of an ocean liner, incorporating the latest technological innovations of the time, and using the work of leading interior designers. English Heritage has set out to recreate the interior as it was when occupied by the Courtaulds in the late 1930s. Most of the furniture and furnishings are replicas of the originals. A variety of attractive woods has been used for panelling. The paintings on display are either copies of works originally there or of works of a similar genre.

The entrance hall leads on one side into the dining-room and on the other side into the drawing-room, alongside which is a corridor leading to the Great Hall; two staircases (in the two front towers) curve up to the first floor. The route through the House now described is as in the audio tour and in Michael Turner's guidebook.

The **entrance hall** is a magnificent space, designed by Rolf Engströmer; it seems circular, but is an equilateral triangle with rounded corners and slightly curved sides. It is lit by an extraordinary lattice-style dome and by a long horizontal window above the door; on either side of the door the panelled wood walls have marquetry paintings by Jerk Werkmäster of, on one side, Swedish buildings with a Viking soldier, and on the other, buildings in Venice and Florence with a Roman soldier. Note the replicas of tub chairs by Engströmer and of the great circular rug by Marion Dorn.

To the right is the **drawing room**, designed by Peter Malacrida. Note the bold white Italian-style fireplace, flanked by green iron window screens; the ceiling beams with Hungarian-style folk decoration; and the panels in the window reveals by Gilbert Ledward. This room may seem rather old-fashioned compared with the more modern style of most of the rest of the house.

Turn left into the corridor with its porthole, and left again into the **boudoir**, designed by Peter Malacrida. Note the long built-in sofa, the ribbed and coved ceiling, and the leather map of South East London, featuring landmarks from Woolwich to Crystal Palace.

Next door is the **library**, also designed by Malacrida, with a cast of the war memorial sculpture The Sentry, by Charles Sargeant Jagger.

At the end of the corridor a doorway leads into the medieval screens passage, with its two adjacent doorways which used to lead into the old buttery and pantry, and then into the Great Hall.

The ***interior** of the **Great Hall** is outstanding; it is one of the finest medieval hall interiors in the country, and has a magnificent timber roof of the hammerbeam type, with a central louvre (now closed) and elaborate pendants.

The hall is an intriguing, and generally successful, mixture of features remaining from the original building (though mainly restored, or rebuilt as virtually identical reproductions), and embellishments added by the Courtaulds during the 1930s.

Apart from the roof, other original features are: the screen at the east end, much restored; and at the west end, the fine stone fan vaulting over the bay windows, and the doorways in the bays which used to lead into the royal apartments.

The minstrels gallery (above the original screen), the canopied screen at the west end, the 10 gondola style lanterns or sconces (recently recreated), and the stained glass by Kruger Gray all belong to the 1930s restoration, and the ornately carved antique (mostly 17th century) furniture was imported at that time. At the west end a door leads into the Orangery.

Back along the corridor. Immediately on reaching the entrance hall, turn left up the west staircase (with its portholes) to the Landing. Here is a copy of a large painting of Sir Stephen and Lady Courtauld with their pet lemur Mah-Jongg, by Campbell Taylor 1934. A corridor to the right leads to the **Minstrels Gallery**, which though historically false provides a spectacular view of the Great Hall.

Back on the landing, **Stephen Courtauld's suite**, designed by John Seely, is immediately to the right. Note the integrated furniture; the Sandersons wallpaper featuring Kew Gardens on opposite walls linked by the white coved ceiling; and the bathroom, tiled largely in blue mosaic.

Next door is the larger and more lavish **Virginia Courtauld's suite**, designed by Malacrida. A circular lobby with curved sliding doors leads into the bedroom, which is circular with two rectangular recesses. The lighting (and central heating) are concealed within the circular ceiling. The bathroom is quite flamboyant, the walls lined with onyx, and the bath set within a gold mosaic niche with a statue of Psyche.

From the landing follow the corridor. Within one of the window bays (corresponding to the Tudor half-timbered gables visible from outside) is a bust of Lady Courtauld by Filippo Locatelli. On reaching Mah-Jongg's quarters (not yet restored), there are good views of the moat and gardens opposite. Further along the corridor, there is a fantastic view of the Tudor gables across the dome of the entrance hall. The corridor winds round to the Venetian Suite and the adjoining Pear Bedroom.

The **Venetian Suite**, not yet fully restored, contains Venetian-style panelling, some of it genuine of the 1780s, a late 17th century Italian tabernacle, and a sunken bath and bidet. The imitation book spines are rather unexpected here. Other guest suites are not open to the public.

Further along the corridor, take the east staircase down to the entrance hall. A doorway to the left leads into the **dining-room**, designed by Malacrida in startling art deco style. Lighting and additional heating is concealed within the aluminium-covered recessed centre of the ceiling. The room is dominated by the black ebonised doors and fireplace panels decorated with ivory-coloured lacquer animals and birds designed by Narini.

A doorway leads to the tea-room (originally the kitchen), shop, and ticket office.

To reach the south side, or garden front, return to the front lawn, then go round the west end of the Great Hall and turn the corner onto the south lawn.

The south lawn covers a network of Tudor courts. A culvert with a Tudor doorway near the orangery provides the best access to the moat *(see below)*. Nearby, beneath a grill set into the lawn is an underground passage (which was a sewer of c1528 leading from the kitchens). The grassed moat on this side is crossed by a timber bridge of the 1930s resting on medieval stone and Tudor brick footings.

The south side of the Great Hall is faced with Kentish ragstone. The south side of Courtauld House adjoining presents a classical facade; the central three bays project slightly, with two Ionic columns and doorways leading into the boudoir and drawing-room, and above are sculptures of Apollo and other figures by Carlton Attwood.

Turn round the corner to the **pergola**, which has three pairs of late 18th century fluted Ionic columns from Sir John Soane's Bank of England, brought here when the Bank was being rebuilt in the 1930s; and the **loggia**, which has Ionic columns and a series of carved stone medallions in relief by Gilbert Ledward. The loggia is under the rear tower at the end of the entrance hall. Beyond, outside the tea room, is the triangular garden, a beautiful parterre planted with herbs; from here there are spectacular views of the rockery and moat. On the east side, as on the south side, the tea room has a similar projecting section with Ionic columns; the sculpture by Attwood represents Domesticity.

The ***gardens** are well worth visiting, being particularly attractive along and around the ***moat**. The gardens and moat are largely as laid out in the late 1930s.

The best access to the moat is from the south lawn, near the orangery at the end of the Great Hall: a Tudor stone doorway leads to a culvert going down - this tunnel is highly atmospheric, it used to connect Henry VIII's apartments to his privy drawbridge (of which there are no remains) across the moat. However, the culvert is not always open. Alternative access to the moat is provided by a slope at the edge of the south lawn, and by a staircase set into the bastion by the triangular garden.

The moat itself remains to the north, the east and (in part) to the west; the remainder is grassed. Basically, the moat wall is made up of 14th century stonework and Tudor brickwork, though much restored (particularly on the east side).

Starting from the Tudor culvert, turn to the right along the west moat wall. The brick buttresses (some with diaper work) were built at the time of the refronting of the royal apartments in the 1580s. From the sunken rose garden, continue through two 'garden rooms' surrounded by shrubs. You come to a formal pool with a fountain, where the moat commences; keep to the outer bank of the moat. The brick upper parts of the buttresses date from the alterations to the queen's apartments c1604. Over the fence to the left can be seen the chauffeur's block and garage c1936 *(see 5A)*.

Bear round to face the north moat wall, keeping to the outer path. You soon come to the moat bridge of the late 1470s *(see page 17)*. The path continues up to the east ridge of the gardens, overlooking the rock garden, the moat and the east moat wall. To the left is a hedged space which was the swimming-pool, and beyond is a pond with an island. Continue round along the ridge until you come to the timber bridge, cross the bridge, then turn right down the slope to the grassed moat area alongside the south moat wall, which retains much 14th century stonework. Continue along the east moat wall, keeping to the path on the inner side of the moat. Take the steps up to the triangular garden, and from there return to the south lawn.

ELTHAM

Gazetteer

Section 'B' CROWN LANDS

(See map on page 22)

Bishop Anthony Bek of Durham granted the manor of Eltham to the Crown in 1305. During the medieval period the Crown lands were very extensive, encompassing most of the land between Shooters Hill in the north and Coldharbour in the south. The only major exception was the Roper Estate at Well Hall *(see page 47)*.

By the Tudor period the northern perimeter of the Palace complex lay broadly along the line of Eltham Hill and the High Street. Nowadays the Crown Estate consists of a core area around the Palace, Court Yard, King John's Walk, Court Road and the Golf Course, together with a number of properties in peripheral areas.

Of the three great royal parklands *(see page 16)*, much of Great Park became the Eltham Golf Course in 1892 and the Royal Blackheath Golf Course in 1923, whilst much of Middle Park and Horn Park were acquired by the then Metropolitan Borough of Woolwich for housing in the 1930s. The fields on either side of King John's Walk were also part of Middle Park.

In the section which follows most locations are still Crown land, other locations remained Crown land until the interwar period.

2. **Lord Chancellor's Lodgings, 34/38 Court Yard. This is the only surviving Tudor building of the Green Court of the Palace. Converted to three houses, it remains highly attractive. Going from north to south, no 34 was the parlour, no 36 (with the oriel window) the Hall, and no 38, the impressive projecting house, the Great Chamber. It was much restored and partly rebuilt in the early 18th century, and again in the early 1950s, using much of the original woodwork and largely maintaining the early 16th century appearance of the frontage of the building. The exterior shows the timber-framing with a continuous overhang; there are later brick extensions at the rear, except for no 38 which has a timber-framed rear. The dormers and the pediment over the oriel are probably 18th century.

*Nos 32/32a, which adjoin to the north, are on the site of a Tudor service building, the buttery. The two houses were restored and partly rebuilt in the early 1950s, respecting the appearance of the previous early 18th century frontage, with the exception of the roughcast facing, which is unfortunate.

3. *Court Yard (southern part). The modern road Court Yard follows the line of an old lane which connected Eltham Palace with the village and parish church. Nowadays its northern part has become like an extension of Court Road.

For the northern part of Court Yard, from the junction with Court Road to Eltham High Street, see 19.

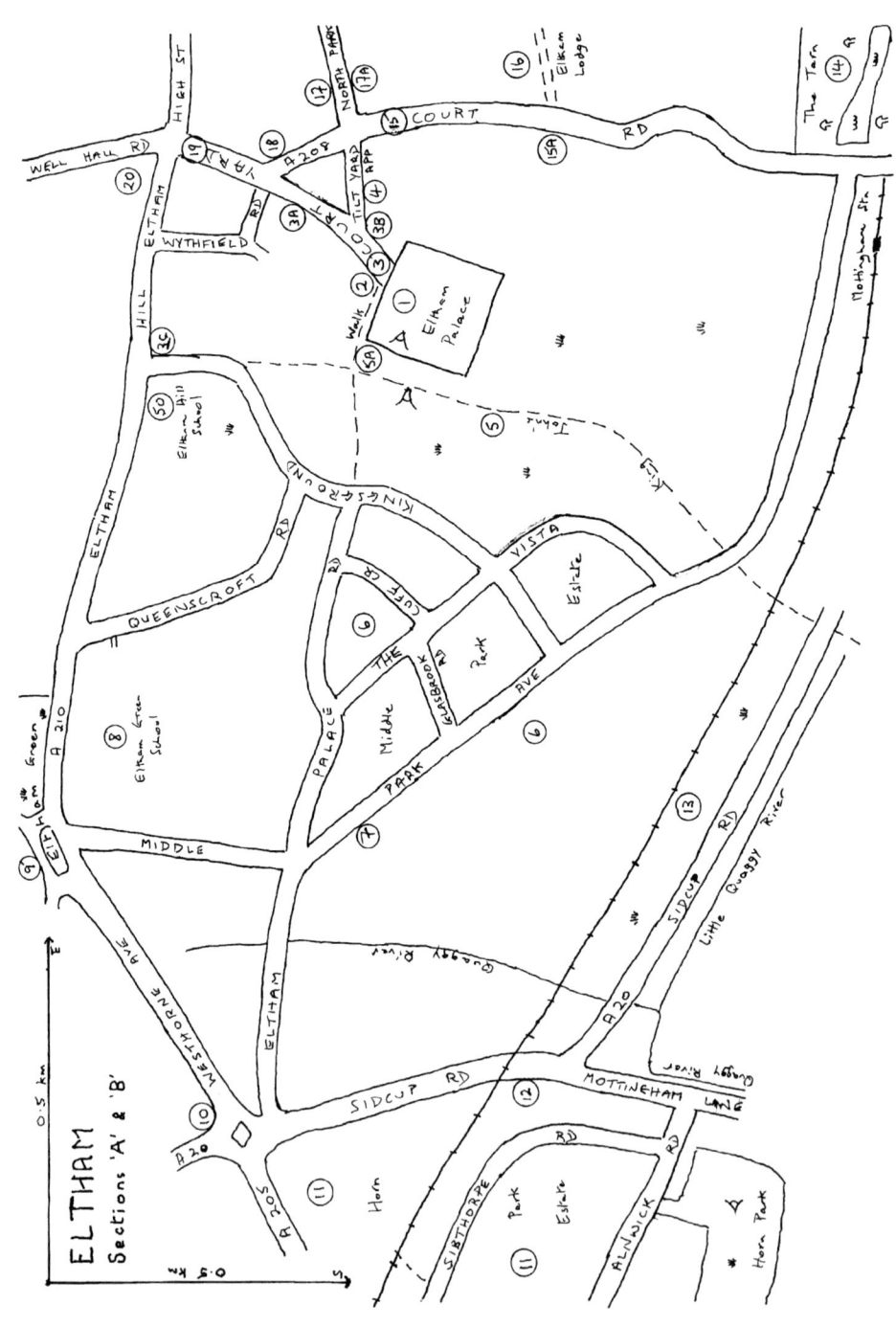

The section of Court Yard from Tilt Yard Approach south to the moat formed the Green Court of Eltham Palace, and still retains something of its atmosphere. On both sides of the road, contributing to this atmosphere, are lengthy stretches of old red brick walling. The date of these walls is uncertain; they may have been erected here in the 18th century, though parts may be older.

The only remaining building of the Green Court is the Lord Chancellor's Lodgings *(see 2)*, on the west side. Nos 32/32a next door, which (apart from the roughcast facing) maintain the appearance of an early 18th century house, are on the site of the Tudor buttery, a service building to the Lodgings. Further north, still on the west side, **Bramber House** and **Orchard House**, were built in 1935 and 1955 respectively on the sites of other service buildings.

The section of Court Yard beyond here, as far as the junction with Wythfield Road and Court Road, was part of the Outer Courtyard of the Palace. First **Chaundrye Close (3A)**, a group of 1959, built on the site of a 17th century house called The Chaundrye. The old red brick wall in front of Chaundrye Close is of particular appeal. Then comes **no 28**, a large detached stock brick house of the late 1860s, with modern extensions.

On the east side of Court Yard, **The Gatehouse (3B)**, a large house with half-timbered gables at the junction with Tilt Yard Approach, is located alongside the site of the original gatehouse to the Green Court. It was built for the novelist Ellen Thorneycroft Fowler in 1914; note the Tudor rose and portcullis designs on the porch.

In Eltham Hill to the north, east of the junction with Kingsground, is a section of walling **(3C)**, which gives an idea of how the original Palace wall would have looked. The legend on a plaque placed there by The Eltham Society reads: 'A wall on this site and to this design formed part of the outer perimeter walling of the original Eltham Palace complex'. Nearby, old walling in front of and in the grounds of Eltham Hill School *(see 50)* originally formed part of walling within the Palace grounds.

4. *Tilt Yard Approach. This short road has an early 16th century gateway and long high walls remaining from the Tudor tiltyard, which was to the east of the Green Court of the Palace. (Further sections of the tiltyard walls can be seen from the Palace car park, *see page 17.*)

The **gateway** retains its Tudor coping. If the gate is open, a smaller Tudor gateway and a stretch of Tudor wall can be seen on the right. The house behind the walls, The Tilt Yard, is of 1931.

5. *King John's Walk. A pleasant and remarkably rural lane, which was an old path through former royal parklands from Eltham to Mottingham; it now forms part of the Green Chain Walk. It starts along the north boundary of Eltham Palace, turns left to skirt the west boundary of the Palace, and passes fields on both sides before reaching Middle Park Avenue; it then goes over the railway to Sidcup Road and on to Mottingham Lane.

The short north section provides a view of the moat, the moat wall and the Palace beyond. At the corner on the left is **1/3 King John's Walk (5A)**, formerly called The Cottage, now converted to flats from a large house built c1936 by Seely & Paget to serve as garages and the chauffeur's block for the Courtauld family *(see also page 20)*. The dormers and the massive brick chimneystacks are attractive features. From here footpaths continue ahead and to the right into Kingsground on the Middle Park Estate, but the Walk itself turns sharp left.

The next section, which is well paved, provides excellent views over South London and towards Central and North London. Beyond this section the Walk can get quite muddy; there is a network of fields on both sides, with no public access. Further on, the Walk goes gradually downhill, with large fields on both sides which do have public access, before reaching Middle Park Avenue near a bridge over the railway.

About half way along the Walk, a branch of the Green Chain Walk leads to the left. It becomes an attractive narrow lane between fine hedgerows before ending up in Middle Park Avenue nearer the junction with Court Road.

Beyond the railway bridge the Walk goes alongside Harmony Wood *(see 13)* and then, on the other side of Sidcup Road, the old Mottingham Farm fields *(see Mottingham 10)*, before reaching Mottingham Lane.

6. Middle Park Estate. This estate was developed from 1931 to 1936; it is well laid out with winding roads and greens. It is located in former royal parkland, with Eltham Palace looming above, and is almost surrounded by fields and open space.

Many of the houses have mock Tudor gables, and this gives parts of the estate a picturesque effect, particularly in **Glasbrook Road**, and also in **Cuff Crescent** and in **Eltham Palace Road**. Middle Park Avenue is the pivotal road, with an outstanding building, St Saviours Church *(see 7)*. The small shopping centre is at the junction of Middle Park Avenue and Kingsground.

The estate contains two of the three surviving examples in Eltham of the **K2 type of red cast-iron telephone kiosk**, designed by Sir Giles Gilbert Scott in 1927 - by the junction of Eltham Palace Road and The Vista, and by the junction of Kingsground and Queenscroft Road. The third is outside the reservoir at the eastern end of Eltham High Street. There are no surviving examples in Eltham of the K6 type of kiosk, designed by Scott in 1935. (The K2 type has all panes of glass of the same size, whereas the K6 type features narrow rectangular panes of glass.)

7. *Church of St Saviour, Middle Park Avenue. A dramatic church of 1933 by Nugent Cachemaille-Day; it is considered as influenced by the German 'expressionist' style of the 1920s, and it was one of the first churches in a modern style in the London area. The dark purple brick exterior with its tall narrow windows has a restless outline. The tower at the east end is in fact the chancel roof, which is higher than the nave roof.

The brick and concrete *interior *(contact the Vicarage next door or phone 020-8850 6829)* has a striking atmosphere, with wonderful light patterns coming through the tall narrow windows, and is full of interest. Note the brick pulpit, lectern and sedilia; the reredos, with a concrete statue of Christ by Donald Hastings; the green hanging crucifix with its strange details; brilliant bright blue stained glass at the east end; and the massive concrete font (probably also by Hastings). The brick pillars and pulpit echo the restless and angular pattern of the exterior. The original windows at the west end were replaced by larger panes with lightly coloured glass by Laurence King in the 1960s. Another lectern, in the nave, and an altar in the Lady Chapel (to the north of the chancel), both of wood, were imported later. Also in the Lady Chapel are a concrete reredos in relief (probably also by Hastings), and some vividly coloured small stained glass windows of the 1970s by John Hayward (one in memory of Bill Hamling, Labour MP for West Woolwich 1964-75; in the corner is an old Gothic stone fragment from Southwark Cathedral. At the west end of the south aisle is the British Legion Chapel (Eltham & Well Hall Branch) 1971.

8. Eltham Green School, Queenscroft Road. A massive modern building of 1956 with splayed wings, which broods over the surrounding area. On the wall of an outbuilding on the east side is **Descending Forms**, an abstract sculpture by Robert Adams.

9. *Eltham Green. This old piece of common land is now split apart by Westhorne Avenue and its roundabout. In a pleasant setting fronting the west part of the Green is a varied and attractive group of houses, mostly of the late 1840s (some with modern porches or extensions). Some are detached houses, others are pairs. The only serious intrusions are a postwar block in the grounds of no 8, and nos 11/12, a pair c1903; otherwise the whole group is very handsome.

The granolithic horse trough of 1916 at the corner of Eltham Green Road was transferred here in 1932 from opposite the pub 'We Anchor in Hope' at the eastern foot of Shooters Hill.

10. Cliftons Service Station. Though restored and altered, this romantic garage of 1936 has retained its great corner archways under great mock-Tudor gables.

11. Horn Park Estate. This well laid out estate was built on former Palace parkland from 1936. Many houses have mock Tudor gables.

There is a small shopping centre on Sibthorpe Road, and from here a lane leads to a footbridge (the only structure pre-dating the estate) across the railway line between Lee and Mottingham, which runs in a cutting through the estate.

To the south, the open space of **Horn Park** provides a good view towards Eltham Palace and Shooters Hill.

12. The Dutch House, Sidcup Road. This roadhouse-type pub of 1939 has prominent 'Dutch' features, including shaped gables in front, stepped gables at the sides, and a plaque of a couple in period dress under orange trees.

13. Harmony Wood is not yet quite a wood, but an extensive oblong of grassland, where in the eastern half clumps of saplings and shrubs have been planted in recent years, mostly by local schoolchildren.

It occupies a sloping site, from the railway line (which is partly in a cutting, partly on an embankment) down to Sidcup Road. The Quaggy River flows through the western end of the field, before going into a tunnel under the railway line. *(For the fields south of Sidcup Road, see Mottingham 10.)*

14. *The Tarn. A beautiful park, with a large lake, a bird sanctuary in dense woodland in the north-east part of the site, and many fine tall trees. The lake has two islands and is crossed by a modern bridge; many types of water-birds can usually be seen. Formerly part of the grounds of Eltham Lodge *(see 16)*, it was acquired by the Metropolitan Borough of Woolwich in 1935.

By the entrance is an *ice-well, a brick structure c1760, sited in a shady spot and formerly used for storing ice (which came from the lake) for Eltham Lodge. A top section has been removed to give a view of the interior.

15. *Court Road. An attractive, winding road with many fine trees, and a number of large late 19th century detached houses, interspersed with modern houses and blocks of flats. The road was constructed after the opening of Mottingham Station in 1866; it followed the line of an old track which led to Chapel Farm in Mottingham. The west side was developed from 1869, the east side from the early 1890s (following the death of Anne Wood, of Eltham Lodge, *see 16*).

Most of the older houses are of yellow brick, a few of red brick. Many have interesting decorative features. Prominent gabled bays and a varied roof outline are common features, otherwise there is a wonderful variety of design.

The most impressive house is **no 62 (15A)** on the west side, now called Parnell House, of 1874. It is very tall with a chequer-board stone entrance stairway leading up to an imposing porch; the gable over the bay windows to the right has a triplet of round-headed windows. Adjacent is the old coach-house.

Going north from no 62, there are a number of other interesting houses on the west side. No 56, called Cathay House, has a decorative porch with columns and a balustraded balcony above; no 58 was its coach-house. No 50 has a big square tower forming a bay to the right. No 46 has a large gabled bay to the right with bargeboarding, and a circular window in a small gable above the recessed porch; no 48, called Langdon House, is similar but the grey brick has been painted red. No 32, called The Beeches, has in its projecting porch a Gothic doorway, an unusual feature here. No 26 is a red brick Arts & Crafts house of 1880, with a jettied tiled gable to the right. Nos 20/24, three stock brick houses, are of 1869, the earliest development in the road. Apart from nos 20/24 and no 26, all these houses are of the 1870s.

On the east side, the houses to the south of the entrance to the Golf Club were built in the early 1890s, the houses to the north were built from c1900.

North of the entrance to the Golf Club, note the following houses, going from north to south. No 21, built c1903, with red brick ground floor and red tiled upper floor, has a neo-Georgian wooden doorcase and a conical roof over a projecting corner bay. No 43 is a bright red brick Arts & Crafts house, probably c1900, with a prominent half-timbered gable and a fine rustic porch facing south with a gabled dormer above. No 47 is a fine Arts & Crafts house, probably c1900, with lots of good decorative features - a distinctive projecting ground floor window and a horizontal window in the gable, a very positive wooden porch with a circular window to its left, and a colonnaded verandah.

South of the entrance to the Golf Club, note the following houses, all of the early 1890s. In no 87, the projecting upper floor windows with gables above are a powerful feature; note also the fine round-headed wooden porch, the gabled south side facing the large walled garden, egg-and-dart moulding over the ground floor windows, and some distinctive woodwork. No 93 has a fine roof with an Arts & Crafts dormer over a large bay with a red brick ground floor bay window. No 99 has a fine pattern of windows set back to the left, and the porch in an angle. No 105 has decorative stonework in a triangular gable over a full-height bay.

16. ***Eltham Lodge. One of the finest classical mansions in London, designed for Sir John Shaw by Hugh May 1664. It was one of the earliest examples of its type in Britain, influenced strongly by earlier Dutch buildings (particularly the Mauritshuis at The Hague). Since 1923 it has been the clubhouse of the Royal Blackheath Golf Club, though it remains Crown property.

> Eltham Palace was, apart from the Great Hall, largely destroyed during the Civil War. The palace lands, including the vast parklands, were leased in 1663 by Charles II to, among others, Sir John Shaw, who had financed him during the Commonwealth period. In 1664 Shaw built Eltham Lodge for himself in the middle of Great Park.

The interior was extensively refurbished c1755. From 1845 to 1889 the tenant of Eltham Lodge was Anne Wood, aunt of Charles Stewart Parnell's mistress Kitty O'Shea, who lived in a now demolished house in North Park nearby. It was due to Mrs Wood's objections that the first railway line to Eltham was, in 1866, routed to the south of Great Park *(see Mottingham 1)*.

The Royal Blackheath Golf Club moved here from Blackheath in 1923 to merge with the Eltham Golf Club, which had occupied the grounds since 1892. The Royal Blackheath is the world's oldest golf club; the oldest golf course is at St Andrews.

As this is a private club, there is no access for the general public. However, visitors with a special interest in viewing the interior may be shown around by prior arrangement; and should contact the Club Secretary on 020-8850 1795.

Visitors wishing just to see the exterior of the building should call at the Secretary's Office, to the left of the entrance hall, and ask for permission.

The building is in red brick, and is harmonious and extremely graceful. The main entrance front facing north is particularly elegant, with its classical doorcase, four giant Ionic pilasters and fine pediment containing swags and a cartouche with coat of arms. The garden front facing south is also highly attractive; the porch was probably added later.

The dentilled cornice, which runs round the front pediment and is continued under the eaves right round the house, is a key feature of the exterior. Note also the blind arched recesses on the side walls, recurring in the centre of the garden front. The hipped roof has a silhouette which is slightly swept-upwards. Each side has two dormers, except the east side, which has one. All the windows are sash windows of the 18th century.

The ***interior** is quite exuberant, well worth visiting if possible *(see above)*, particularly to see the Main Staircase, the Secretary's Office, and the O'Shea Room. The interior was extensively restored c1755, and much of the internal furnishings, particularly fireplaces and plasterwork, dates from that time.

The front entrance leads straight into the **Hall**, which has a screen of two pairs of Ionic columns (added in the 19th century) separating it from the Inner Hall and the two staircases. Beyond the Inner Hall is the **Ante-Room**, which leads to the garden porch. The rooms of principal interest on the ground floor are on either side of the Hall, and on either side of the Ante-Room.

To the left of the Hall is the **Secretary's Office** (originally the parlour). This is sumptuously decorated, with very lovely and quite elaborate rococo plasterwork of the mid 18th century on the walls and ceiling. There is a fine wooden chimneypiece, the upper part with a framed painting of a classical scene.

To the right of the Hall is the **Nineteenth Hole**, a small bar, with a pleasing wooden fireplace.

To the left of the Ante-Room is the **Ladies Lounge** (originally the breakfast-room) with an elegant chimneypiece and intricate plasterwork on the ceiling.

To the right of the Ante-Room is the **Bar** (originally the Dining Room), with an extraordinary mid 18th century chimneypiece of white and pink Carrara marble - note the carved rams on either side of a carved panel showing cherubs shearing a sheep.

The **Main Staircase** is to the right of the Inner Hall and retains the original woodwork; it has fantastic and intricate carving, with pine panels of foliage and cherubs, and newel posts topped by floral urns. The ceiling has, amongst ample plasterwork, a very densely carved oval garland which formerly framed a painting. On the walls are portraits of Sir John Shaw and family attributed to Sir Peter Lely.

The rooms of principal interest on the upper floor are the Billiard Room, the Captain's Room, and the O'Shea Room.

To the left of the landing is the **Billiard Room**, with a marble chimneypiece and intricate plasterwork on the ceiling, which is original. Note the great fluted Corinthian pilasters at the west end, remaining from a screen of columns.

Leading off the billiard room to the right is the **Captain's Room**, with an elegant plasterwork ceiling, and finely carved doorcase, chimneypiece and frieze.

To the right of the landing is the **Dining Room** (originally the Grand Parlour), with very densely carved plasterwork on the ceiling.

Opposite the head of the Main Staircase is a door leading to a corridor, off which to the left is the **O'Shea Room**, so-called because of associations with Kitty O'Shea *(see page 27)*. This small room, beautiful and refined, is divided by a finely carved round-arched part-screen resting on Corinthian columns. There is a fine chimneypiece, surmounted by a handsomely framed painting of St Jerome. Both screen and chimneypiece are of the mid 18th century.

From the corridor a secondary staircase leads to a **museum** in the attic, containing 18th and 19th century golf clubs, golfing trophies etc, as well as the original lease of 1663 granting the Manor of Eltham to Sir John Shaw and others.

The house is in the middle of the golf course; the grounds, particularly to the south, are vast and magnificent. There are belts of woodland both to the east and the west of the house. In the woodland to the east is a large pond. In the north-east of the grounds is a lovely, smaller pond, surrounded by willow trees; this pond is famous for its population of great crested newts. *For The Tarn, accessible to the public, see 14.*

Near the house are sections of brick wall, parts of which are probably 17th century. Also to the east is a cottage, of 17th century structure but substantially altered and extended in the early 19th century; adjoining this to the south is an early 19th century wooden garden pavilion.

17. North Park. Of this long street, the eastern part was laid out with large houses in the late 1860s, but these have disappeared to make way for postwar blocks of flats. The western part was laid out c1903; of this period, nos 5 and nos 9/15, large houses with polygonal bay windows, remain. Of special interest is

4 North Park (17A), in a former orchard. Designed by Nicholas Burwell 1998 for his own use, modern but restrained, no way discordant in the street. Red brick with a white section to the right and a rectangular timber box projecting over the entrance.

18. Eltham United Reformed Church, Court Road, a red brick building of 1936. It has a tall Gothic entrance, with lancets above a tier of recessed arches. Ask at the caretaker's house behind to see the **interior**, dominated by its great chancel arch.

> This is Eltham's fourth Congregational Church. The first was built in Sun Yard 1799, and closed c1835. The second, in Georgian style, was built on the site of Eltham Arcade 1839. The third was built at the junction of Well Hall Road and the High Street in 1868, in a strong Gothic style with a tall spire; it was demolished in 1936 when the Court Road church was built, and. the site became Burtons *(see 21A)*.

19. Court Yard (northern part). See also 3. The section of this street between the High Street and Wythfield Road now seems like an extension to Court Road. On the west side, nos 18/26 are an impressive group of detached stock brick houses of the mid 1860s. On the east side, nos 5/9 are a terrace of 1810, with modern shopfronts.

ELTHAM

Gazetteer

Section 'C' HIGH STREET & SOUTHEND
(See map on page 30)

20. *Church of St John the Baptist. A large Victorian Gothic ragstone church of 1875 designed by Sir Arthur Blomfield. Originally the tower and spire of the previous church were retained, but they were considered incongruous and were replaced by the present dominant tower and broach spire in 1879. The large extension to the north is the vestry, of 1988.
> The first record of a church on the site is c1160, and the burial ground is probably at least as old as this. It was the original parish church of Eltham. The second known church was built in the 17th century; its tower was on the site of the present tower, but the nave was to its east, ie to the south of the present nave. This church is the third on the site; it was substantially restored by Thomas Ford after damage in the last war.

The *interior is of considerable interest *(the church is often open in the morning, otherwise contact the Vicarage, Sowerby Close, or phone 020-8859 1242)*. The overall impression, largely the result of re-ordering by Thomas Ford, is simple and spacious; the whitewashed rendering emphasises the boldness of the Gothic arcades, and the postwar stained glass at both ends makes the whole effect bright and colourful. The stained glass at the east end is traditional, by Sir Ninian Comper, whereas at the west end it is more modern with vivid colours, by B.E. Barber 1953. The only prewar stained glass windows to survive are in the north aisle, by Burlison & Grylls, and in the lady chapel. The timber roof of the nave and aisles is imposing.

Inside the porch, set into the wall on the right at ground level by the entrance door, is a square stone marked with a cross; this is part of a 12th century sarcophagus, the only survival from the first church on the site. Remaining from the second church are: a number of wall monuments and memorial tablets, 18th and 19th century, some quite pleasing, along both aisles (note Arthur Pott 1823 by John Bacon the Younger at the east end of the north aisle); an early 19th century royal coat of arms on the west wall; and an early 19th century brass lectern. The pulpit is of 1875.

The nave pews are Victorian; they were imported in 1974 from St Marys Lambeth (which became the Museum of Garden History). There is a chair of 1625 (a modern gift) in the sanctuary.

The **churchyard**, particularly the old burial ground to the north, is ancient. The walls to the south and east are in part 17th century. The south wall incorporates the Eltham war memorial cross, of 1924, as well as a drinking fountain of 1886; behind the wall is a raised walkway parallel with the road. The lych-gate in the south-east corner was erected in 1881. On the south wall of the church is a board commemorating the burial nearby in 1721 of Thomas Doggett, actor-manager and founder of the Doggetts Coat & Badge Race for young watermen which is held on the Thames every summer.

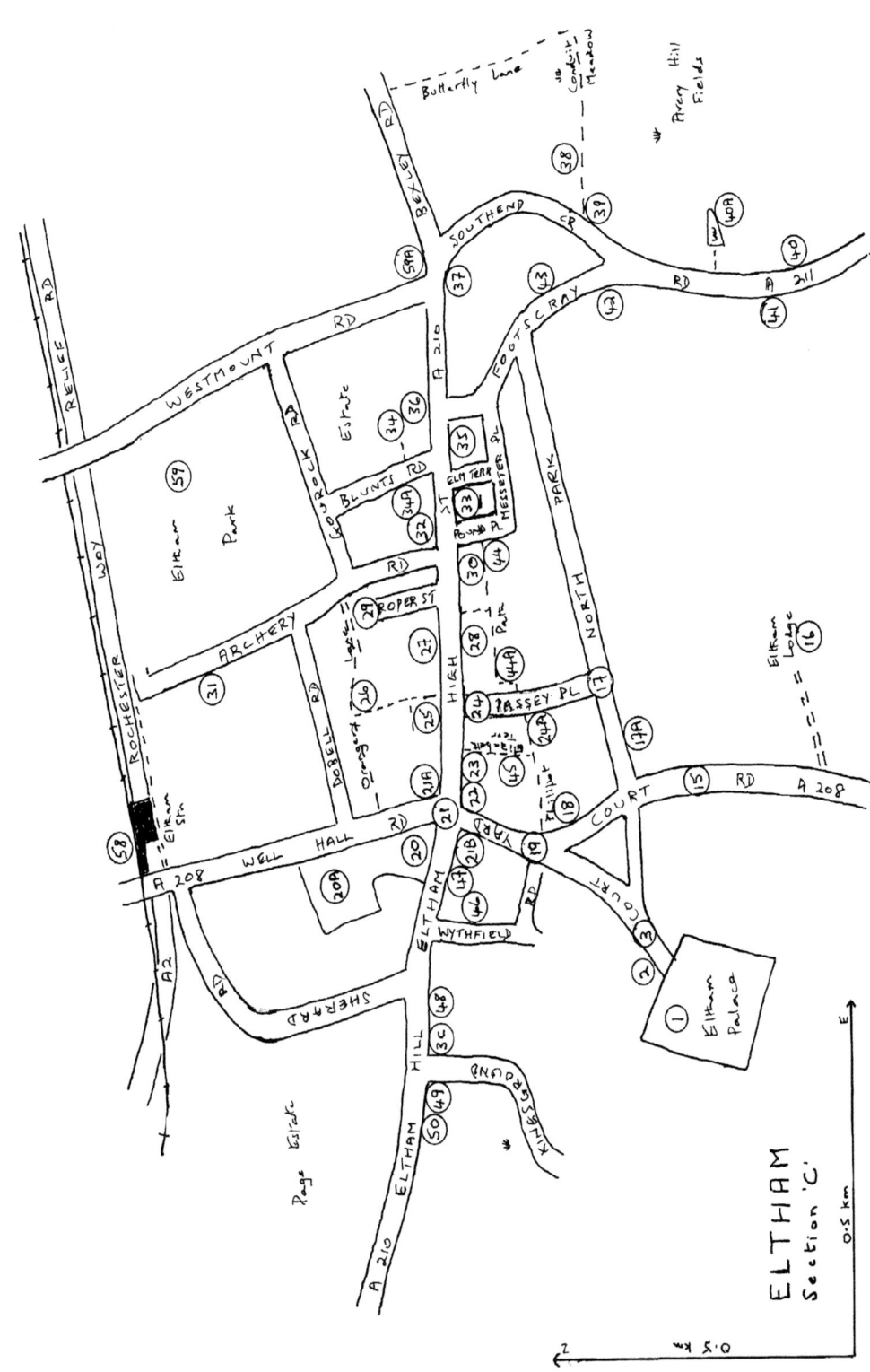

The *burial ground (20A) is wild and wonderful, crammed with old tombs, mainly 18th and 19th century, but the ground is uneven in places and some care should be taken when walking around. By the east wall, alongside the pathway into Well Hall Road, is a tombstone 1794 to Yemmerrawanyea Kebbarah, one of the first two Australian aborigines to visit Europe (he returned with Admiral Arthur Philip, the first Governor of New South Wales, in 1792). Slightly to the north, in the centre of the burial ground, is a large tomb-chest with vermiculated sides to Sir William James 1783, the naval commander commemorated by Severndroog Castle *(see Shooters Hill 8)*. Further north are two prominent tombs close to each other - one is to John North 1898, of Avery Hill *(see 52)*, and the other, an obelisk, to the family of William Blenkiron 1871, whose famous stud farm was on the site of the Middle Park Estate.

21. High Street crossroads. In addition to the church, the other buildings at the junction of the High Street with Well Hall Road and Court Yard are of interest.

McDonalds (21A) occupies a handsome building with great Ionic columns and pilasters at first floor level; it was built as a Burtons shop in 1937 *(see also 18)*. Next door is **NatWest Bank**, no 65, handsome neo-Georgian red brick, of 1922.

The Banker's Draft, opposite at 80 Eltham High Street, is of 1931, refurbished and converted from a Barclays Bank branch to a Wetherspoon pub 1993. It contains mementos of the comedian Frankie Howerd, who spent his youth in Eltham.

76/78 Eltham High Street (21B) form a distinctive group of shops of 1926, Tudor half-timbered with five white gables. Adjoining, nos **64/74** are another interesting group, of 1928, neo-Georgian red brick in the centre, flanked by two pairs with long sloping roofs and dormers.

22. *The Greyhound, 86 Eltham High Street, now called Ye Olde Greyhound. A brick village-style pub, partly rebuilt in 1978, with the exterior conforming closely to its previous appearance of 1720. In the ground floor bar is a stone Tudor fireplace, with later Dutch tiling, possibly brought from Eltham Palace. The bar also contains extraordinary lifesize waxwork models of 1998 of a greyhound and some racing fans, as well as other greyhound racing memorabilia.

23. *Mellins, 90 Eltham High Street. An attractive shop, basically c1720, weatherboarded side and rear, with an unusual mid 19th century shopfront. Formerly a pharmacy, it has been nicely converted to a wine bar.

24. Passey Place is part pedestrianised, with some interesting buildings.

At the top is the **Eltham town sign**, erected by The Eltham Society 1993, designed by Paul Cookson, featuring local buildings. There is also a town centre map, one of several in the town centre.

The Old Post Office, no 4, handsomely converted to a pub in 1995. It was in fact originally a Post Office, a neo-classical building of 1912, the right-hand part being added in 1935 - note the ornamented pediment and royal insignia over the doorway.

The Park Tavern, no 45. The building is basically mid 19th century, though its present appearance is late 19th century, with Trumans green tiling c1910.

Eltham and Mottingham House (24A), no 32. A handsome building of 1898, with red brick ground floor and tile-hung upper floor. It was built as the Eltham and Mottingham Cottage Hospital, and is now a home for the elderly.

25. *Cliefden, 97/101 Eltham High Street. A house c1720 with a good fanlight, but spoilt by the roughcast facing and the modern shopfronts. It is not easy to appreciate from close-up that this is an old house; a better perspective can be obtained from Passey Place opposite. The original upper floor windows remain, apart from the first floor window above the entrance which is modern. The **interior** incorporates some 17th century structure, including a fine carved wooden staircase. Next door at no 103 is a mid 19th century extension.

Go down Merlewood Place, the footpath alongside no 105, and into the yard on the left to view the rear, which has original brickwork and a fine fanlight. The yard also leads to the **stables**, a red brick building with tiny chimney and bellcote; it is of early 18th century appearance, though the ground floor may incorporate some 17th century structure.

26. **The Orangery, Orangery Lane. A very elegant red brick structure of c1720; it was the end-piece of the garden of Eltham House, which fronted the High Street until it was demolished in 1937. The tall baroque frontispiece has a broken pediment, elaborate stone carving, and a mask over a central arch.

It is very dilapidated, and at present difficult if not impossible to see, as it is covered by scaffolding and sheeting; several attempts at restoration (which would involve the creation of offices alongside to the west) have been frustrated, and one can only hope that a current project will succeed. It is accessible from the High Street by a footpath alongside no 105, and also from the car park behind Marks & Spencer.

Behind is **Orangery Lane**, a footpath leading to Well Hall Road; this formed part of a much older lane.

27. Barclays Bank, 131 Eltham High Street. A handsome neo-Georgian brick building of 1932, with an imposing stone doorcase.

An ornamental iron gate alongside frames a path leading to **no 131b**, a house of the 1820s in a secluded location; it is now used as offices.

Note the balustrades over the adjacent single storey shops; the shops were erected in the early 1920s, when the High Street was widened. There are similar balustrades and classical parapets over other single storey shops on the High Street further west.

28. 132/136 Eltham High Street is a strange building erected for the grocers David Greig in 1905 - the initials are in terracotta in the gables. Note the fine brickwork, the two balconies, and lots of quirky detail. No 130 adjoining, with its white upper floor, dates back to the mid 19th century.

Further along **nos 146/150**, a red brick building, has dates in each of the three gabled bays - 1653, 1983, 1822. This indicates that the first building was here in 1653, and that it was rebuilt in 1822; it was rebuilt again in 1983, though retaining the broad outline of the earlier building.

29. Eltham Church of England School, Roper Street. A pleasant school building with a multi-gabled facade, bellcote and strange chimneystacks, its location closing the view from the High Street. It was the village school, built 1868, extended 1910.

The houses with bay windows in Roper Street, which are identical on both sides of the street, are c1870.

Moat bridge, Eltham Palace (late 1470s) - *Eltham 1*

Courtauld House (Seely & Paget, 1934-36) - *Eltham 1*

**Lord Chancellor's Lodgings
(early 16th century)
& 32 Court Yard
(early 18th century)**
- *Eltham 4*

**Gateway, Tilt Yard Approach
(early 16th century)**
- *Eltham 4*

Church of St Saviour (Nugent Cachemaille-Day, 1933) - *Eltham 7*

Eltham Green (late 1840s) - *Eltham 9*

Eltham Lodge (Hugh May, 1664), front - *Eltham 16*

Eltham Lodge (Hugh May, 1664), rear - *Eltham 16*

Church of St John the Baptist (Sir Arthur Blomfield, 1874, 1879) - *Eltham 20*

The Greyhound (1720) - *Eltham 22*

Cliefden (c1720) - *Eltham 25*

The Orangery (c1720) - *Eltham 26*

Eltham Library (Maurice Adams, 1906) - *Eltham 32*

The Rising Sun (1904) - *Eltham 32*

Holy Trinity Church (George Street 1869, Sir Arthur Blomfield & Son 1909) - *Eltham 39*

Southend House (17th / early 18th / early 19th century) - *Eltham 40*

Avery Hill gatehouse (Thomas Cutler, 1890) - *Eltham 52A*

Southwood House (late 18th century) - *Eltham 52G*

Greenholm Road (developer Cameron Corbett, c1900-03) - *Eltham 59*

Tudor Barn, Well Hall (16th century) - *Eltham 69C*

Progress Estate, Ross Way (Sir Frank Baines, 1915) - *Eltham 72*

Progress Estate, Well Hall Road (Sir Frank Baines, 1915) - *Eltham 72*

West Park (1887-89) - *Mottingham 3*

Gefferys Court (George Hubbard, 1912) - *Mottingham 16*

Theobalds Cottages (at least 1760s) - *New Eltham 16*

37 Kidbrooke Grove (Sir Reginald Blomfield, 1905) - *Kidbrooke 6*

7/33 Shooters Hill Road (possibly Michael Searles, 1840) - *Kidbrooke 10A*

141/155 Shooters Hill Road (1846) - *Kidbrooke 10E*

Severndroog Castle (Richard Jupp, 1784) - *Shooters Hill 8*

Christ Church (1856) & Ypres milestone - *Shooters Hill 2*

Water Tower (1910) - *Shooters Hill 18*

Former Shooters Hill Fire Station (1912) - *Shooters Hill 21*

30. St Mary's Centre, 180 Eltham High Street. A stately early 19th century house, with deep eaves and a deeply recessed doorway. It was restored to become a community centre in 1986.

> This house was in existence by 1837, when it was let to the Goschen family. Lord Goschen, who was brought up here, became Chancellor of the Exchequer. In 1870 it became a convent school, with two rooms used as a chapel; this marked the beginning of the Roman Catholic revival in Eltham. The first church, St Mary's, opened alongside in 1890; a much larger building, Christ Church, opened further along the High Street in 1912 *(see 36)*. In 1928 the school was renamed St Mary's School, with additional buildings nearby. In 1984 it moved to larger premises in Glenure Road *(see 66)*, and St Mary's Centre is the only building remaining.

31. 55 Archery Road. This house has a Greater London Council blue plaque to the Labour politician Herbert Morrison, Lord Morrison of Lambeth, 1888-1965, cabinet minister and Leader of the London County Council, who lived here 1929-60. The house is of 1929, and is one of a long group of houses with distinctive brickwork.

32. *Eltham Library, Eltham High Street. An impressive Edwardian baroque building of 1906, built with funds from the Carnegie Trust to a design by Maurice Adams. The classical frontispiece is recessed, and on either side are oriel windows and tile-hung gables flanked by urns.

Next door at nos 183-5 is the **Eletriq Cafe**; it has fine half-timbered Tudor upper floors with two-storey oriels and strong gables. This was originally an electricity showroom, built in the early 1930s by the Metropolitan Borough of Woolwich; upstairs at that time was the office of the Council's Registrar. Behind is a building which was used from the early 1900s as electricity works, Woolwich Council being the electricity supply authority at that time.

Next door is **The Rising Sun**, 189 Eltham High Street, a pub of 1904 with a dramatic front, dominated by large bow windows extending through three storeys. Attractive interior, with fine etched glass.

These three buildings form an attractive and interesting sequence.

33. Eltham Arcade, Eltham High Street. Built 1930, intended to be part of a larger development. Note the glazed roof, and classical columns along the upper floor.

34. Fifteenpenny Fields. This group of buildings, belonging to an ancient charity associated with a gift of land by Henry VII in 1492, occupies a secluded position off Blunts Road.

The central almshouse is a very classical building with a very large pediment, surprisingly built as late as 1963. It is difficult to see because of the annexe in front, Thurland House, built in 1989. Adjacent to the main building is a long one-storey terrace, also of 1963, fronting a pleasant green, in the middle of which is an old water standpipe, which used to be on the High Street.

Opposite are **3/7 Blunts Road (34A)**, formerly almshouses of the Philipot charity *(see 44A)*, built in 1872.

35. Eltham Fire Station, 224/8 Eltham High Street. An austere classical red brick building of 1904. But it incorporates, in total contrast, an amazing former pub, **Man of Kent**, of 1888, with an odd corner spire and all sorts of quirky details.

36. Christ Church Presbytery, Eltham High Street. The front of this large house, formerly known as Eagle House, is early 19th century and quite elegant, though rather spoilt by some later additions.

It is worth calling at the Priory and asking for permission to see the rear; looking from the garden it becomes clear that there are really two houses - the house to the east is of red brick and is 18th century, and the house to the west is of yellow brick and is early 19th century, at which time the front was unified. This is the only old garden remaining in the High Street. The red brick garden wall, to the north and east, is 18th century.

The presbytery adjoins **Christ Church**, a Roman Catholic Church in Gothic style by Scoles & Raymond of 1912, extended south to the High Street 1936. The church is of yellow brick and largely symmetrical, with crenellated aisles. The interior *(call at the Priory, or phone 020-8850 1646)* has a powerful chancel arch, fine arcades, and brilliantly colourful stained glass by Harry Clark of Dublin. *See also 30.*

Adjoining the presbytery to the east is **Christ Church Priory**, by F G Broadbent & Partners 1964; on the wall is a sculpted roundel of Christ in Glory by James Butler.

37. Southend Crescent. Nos 2/14, which follow neatly the curve in the road, are a group of houses of the 1840s - nos 2/6 and nos 8/10 (Elm Villas) form a stuccoed terrace, and nos 12/14 (Madras Villas) are a brick pair with a double doorcase and sharing a pediment. Most of these houses have nice bracketed door and window cases, and other ornamental embellishments.

Further along on the west side, **nos 18/20** are a much larger mid 19th century pair, with similar doorcases and two-storey bay windows. **No 32** and **Oakfield**, no 36, are impressive late 19th century detached red brick houses with prominent gables. At the foot of the crescent are **nos 70/72**, a pair, and **no 74**, detached, late 19th century.

38. *Conduit Head. A red brick Tudor structure, which housed sluices controlling the water supply for Eltham Palace and its moat, originating from springs now on Eltham Warren Golf Course. It is accessible a short way along the footpath to the north of Holy Trinity Church.

Beyond, a footpath leads after some distance to **Conduit Meadow**, a pleasant small open space, and from here footpaths continue ahead into Avery Hill Park, and to the left up Butterfly Lane alongside Pippenhall Meadows *(see 51)* to Bexley Road.

39. *Holy Trinity Church, Southend Crescent. A Victorian Gothic ragstone church of 1869 designed by George Street. Substantial alterations were undertaken by the firm of Sir Arthur Blomfield & Son in 1909, when the nave was extended by two bays to the west in identical style, and the south chapel, a dominant baptistry apse and two new porches were added. The present entrance, shared with a new church hall, was part of a major re-ordering by Paul Velluet in 1989, the original Gothic entrance archway of Street's church being repositioned here; the new entrance marks the western limit of the original Street church.

The **interior** *(the church is normally open 1000 to 1100 Wednesday mornings, otherwise contact the vicarage behind the church, or phone 020-8850 1246)* was transformed by the Blomfield alterations of 1909 and by subsequent refurnishings, and nothing of Street's furnishings survives. It is highly decorated and lavish, with an abundance of stained glass.

The three postwar windows along the north aisle are distinctive - the central one by Whitefriars Studio, those on either side by Margaret Cowell. Note also the west window above the entrance to the baptistry apse, in memory of John North of Avery Hill 1909 *(see 52)*; this and other windows in the apse, as well as the fine stencil work on the ceiling, were by the firm of C.E. Kempe. The south aisle windows are by Whitefriars Studio of the 1950s. It is worth asking for help in finding the two porches added in 1909, for each contains a fine window by Kempe portraying an angel with a musical instrument. In the chancel the east window is by Whitefriars (based on a design by Kempe).

The flamboyant reredos is by W. D. Caröe c1904. The tabernacle and, at the crossing, the altar and ambo, all with imaginative modern woodwork, are by Velluet.

The south chancel chapel of 1909 was converted in 1917 to become the Gallipoli Memorial Chapel and dedicated as a permanent memorial to those who died in the Gallipoli campaign of 1915; it has a beautifully carved altarpiece, and inscriptions, shields and tablets commemorating the various national forces and the regiments which fought in that campaign. The south window is prewar by Kempe, the east window postwar by Whitefriars. The finely carved font outside the chapel was moved here by Velluet in 1989 from the baptistry apse, which then became a narthex.

The **vicarage** is behind the church; the original building by Street c1870 was in alignment with the present entrance porch. Extensions further west are c1909.

40. *Southend House, 141 Footscray Road. The west front, facing the road, of this attractive red brick house is of early 18th century appearance. Parts of the walls facing north and south, including the curved gables over the entrance, may be 17th century. The house was extended to the east in the early 19th century, and much rebuilt at that time.

It was substantially restored in 1988 to form the central feature of a new housing development. The entrance portico to the north was added as part of the restoration, and is a replica of an old portico which was added in the early 19th century.

Two mid 19th century buildings in the grounds were converted for incorporation into the development - the stables right at the rear, white timbered with some pointed windows, and the lodge, no 145, to the south.

Just to the north of Southend House is a late 18th century **milestone** erected by the New Cross Turnpike Trust, with early 19th century iron plates reading '9 miles to London Bridge, 3 miles to Foots Cray'. *See also Eltham 47, New Eltham 11.*

Further north is the **LESSA pond (40A)**, by the entrance to the London Electricity sports ground. It is a large and attractive pond, surrounded by tall trees, and is supervised by the London Wildlife Trust. It was formerly part of a much larger lake in the grounds of Southend House.

41. 144 Footscray Road. A house of early 18th century structure, with a later extension and a modern porch.

42. 48/60 Footscray Road. This bold neo-classical office development of 1985-90 for the builders Bryen & Langley is in front of an old motorcoach garage.

43. 33/59 Footscray Road, a group of imposing stock brick houses of the late 1860s, with interesting and varied decorative features. No 59, painted white, one of a pair which is more restrained than the others, has a Greater London Council blue plaque to Richard Jefferies, 1848-1887, naturalist and writer, who lived here 1884-85.

44. Philipot Path. This old lane makes its way parallel to the High Street for half a kilometre, between Court Yard and Elm Terrace; it crosses roads and passes through shopping developments, but retains in parts a certain atmosphere.

Going from east to west, after the Sainsbury development, you come to **no 4**, an early 19th century white weatherboarded house, much restored. Next door are **nos 1/2**, late 19th century cottages, much altered.

In the central section is **Thomas Philipot Almshouses (44A)**, built as two blocks 1929 and 1930, and extended to form a long terrace 1978, with separate blocks of flats of 1979 and 1983. On the wall at the west end is a tablet of 1694 removed from the original almshouses which were in the High Street near Blunts Road. Above the old plaque is the tercentenary sundial 1694-1994, installed 1995. (In the Greenwich Borough Museum at Plumstead Library is a wooden door from the original almshouses of 1694.)

Further west, beyond Passey Place, are **nos 23/24**, probably c1840, similar to the adjacent Elizabeth Terrace *(see below)*, though with the addition of doorcases.

45. Elizabeth Terrace. This footpath embodies a strange phenomenon - the footway separates the terraced cottages c1840 from their own front gardens.

46. Bob Hope Theatre, Wythfield Road. A building of 1910, which was originally the parish hall for the Church of St John the Baptist *(see 20)*. It became Eltham Little Theatre in 1946, and was renamed Bob Hope Theatre in 1982. The four prominent Tuscan columns on the frontage relieve an otherwise rather dismal facade. The interior is highly attractive. (Bob Hope was born at 44 Craigton Road on the Eltham Park Estate, *see 59B*.)

Alongside, **1/3 Wythfield Road** are three detached stock brick houses, c1866.

47. The Chequers, 34 Eltham High Street. An agreeable pub of 1903, with half-timbered bargeboarded gables. Attached to the front is an 18th century **milestone** erected by the New Cross Turnpike Trust, with early 19th century iron plates reading '8 miles to London Bridge, 4 miles to Foots Cray'. *See also 40, New Eltham 11.*

48. *Queenscroft, 150 Eltham Hill. A fine red brick house c1720, linked to a larger neo-Georgian block of 1973 in yellow brick.

49. Mecca Bingo, Eltham Hill. A rather alarming art deco building in startling colours, built as an Odeon cinema by Andrew Mather 1938. It has been a bingo hall since 1967.

50. Eltham Hill School, Eltham Hill. The original building of 1927 cannot be seen from the road, though the rear range can be seen from the recreation ground in Queenscroft Road. *(Ask at the Secretary's office for permission to look round.)*

The modern purple brick buildings fronting Eltham Hill are of 1975. The games hall, the prominent brick building to the right, is lit by a bold projecting clerestory.

Behind the frontage, on the west and south sides of a quadrangle, is the original building of 1927. At the back, to the south-west of the main buildings, is the New Block, modernist with layers of glass and brick, by Trevor Dannatt 1969.

The buildings occupy part of the original grounds of Eltham Palace. To the west (visible from the main road) is a small late 17th century brick **garden house**, at present in rather poor condition. The adjoining walls and the boundary wall in front of the school may also date from the 17th century.

ELTHAM

Gazetteer

Section 'D' AVERY HILL

(See map on page 38)

51. *Pippenhall Meadows. Originally part of Pippin Hall Farm, these fields are amongst the oldest in Eltham. They became part of the Avery Hill Estate in the 1890s, and are now used by riding stables and as allotments. There is public access only to the large easternmost field on Bexley Road.

There are public footpaths on either side of the Meadows; they form part of the Green Chain Walk, and are for the most part highly attractive. The footpath to the east is quite delightful; much of it is flanked by tall and ancient hedgerows, and it continues through to Avery Hill Park. The footpath to the west, Butterfly Lane, leads to Conduit Meadow *(see 38)*.

The low-lying area in the southern part of the Meadows is an area of wetland, containing the source of the River Shuttle, which flows into the River Cray near Hall Place, Bexley.

On Bexley Road near the beginning of the footpath is an old **milestone** with the inscription '9 miles to London Bridge, 7 miles to Dartford'.

52. *Avery Hill. The large and luxurious mansion of Avery Hill was built in vast grounds in 1890 for John North; it was in a flamboyant renaissance style, and the architect was Thomas Cutler. Much of it was destroyed in the last war, and what remains is rather overshadowed by postwar additions and extensions, but it is a fascinating though rather jumbled complex. It is now the Avery Hill Campus of the University of Greenwich, though the Winter Garden (a conservatory at the rear) and the Park are open to the public.

> John North made a fortune out of the nitrate trade in Chile. He acquired the estate of Avery Hill in 1883; it then contained a mansion of c1841. In 1888 North demolished this house, retaining only one small room, and built a much larger mansion, completed in 1890, to demonstrate his extravagant life-style. He also set up a stud farm to the west, and a 'model farm' to the north. While his new mansion was being built, he lived in Southwood House to the south.
>
> North lived at Avery Hill for only a few years, for he died in 1896. The estate was acquired by the London County Council in 1902; the grounds became a public park, and in 1906 the buildings (apart from the Winter Garden) became London's first residential teachers training college, then for women only. It is now an integral part of the University of Greenwich, which has plans for considerable expansion on the site.

The *****gatehouse (52A)** on Bexley Road is at the western end of the complex. It has a remarkable chateau-like roof and fine brick vaulting, and with the adjoining lodge, is of 1890. The lengthy wall of red brick along the north boundary was constructed in 1890 after Bexley Road had been diverted away from its previous route, which was considered by North to be too near his house.

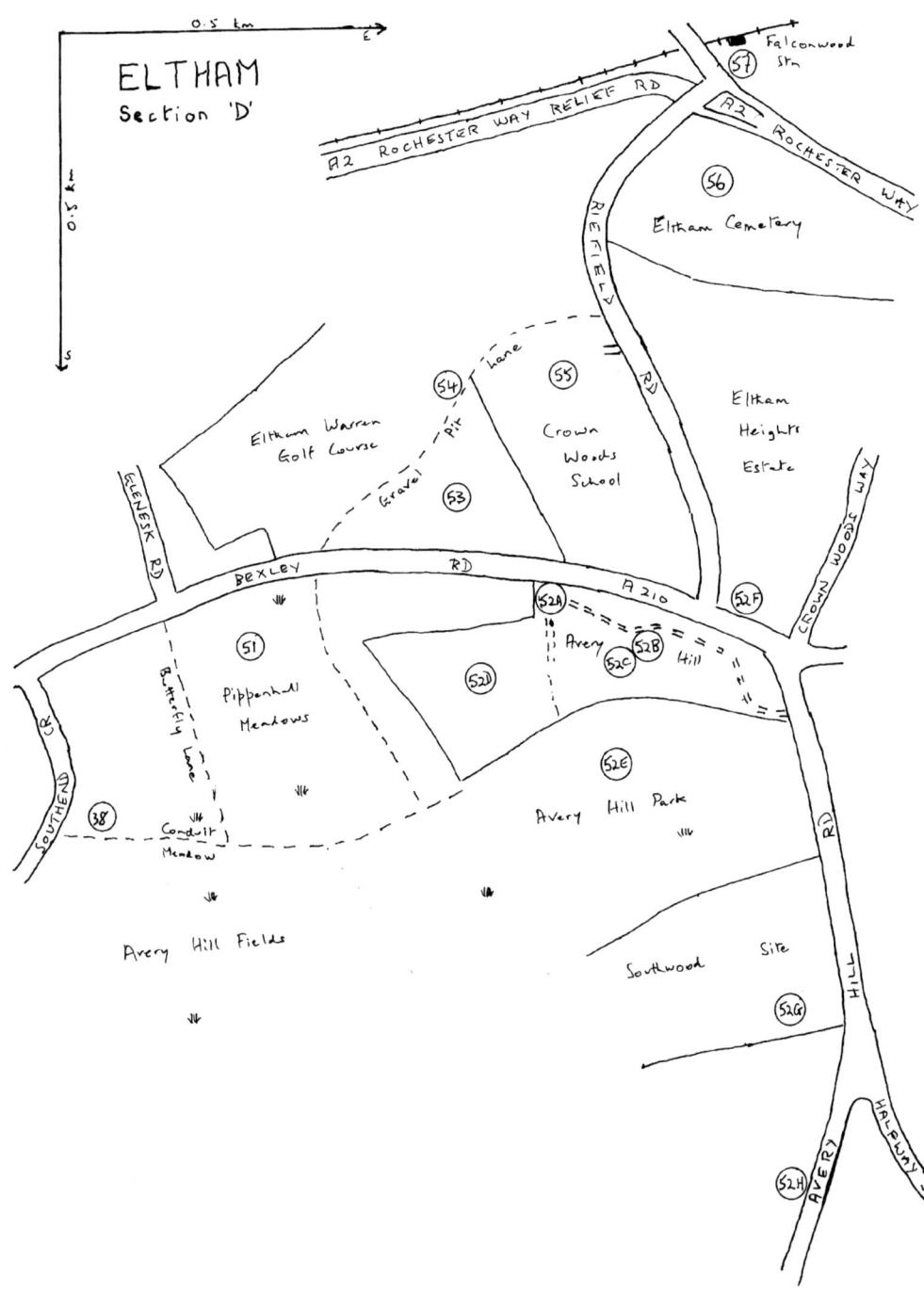

The driveway follows the line of the old Bexley Road, and leads to the entrance front of *Avery Hill Mansion (52B), which faces north. Looking at the exterior, what remains of the 1890 building is basically the large balustraded entrance porte-cochere, and the western part of the Mansion. Other buildings to the west are mainly postwar, though the stables (substantially extended) and the water tower are original. The eastern part of the Mansion and the buildings further east are postwar.

The sequence of buildings along the driveway, from the gatehouse eastwards to Avery Hill Road, is as follows:

(i) The Design and Technology Building, a building of 1963 with a series of sharply angled roofs.

(ii) The Schools of Education and Health, the core of which is the original stables of 1890. The **Stable Block** is the section to the right, with the cupola on top; the section to the left of deeper red brick is an extension of 1907. The wings to the south are postwar additions; the easternmost wing, with its honeycomb-like cladding, of 1961, is very prominent, and gives the name **Honeycomb Building** to the complex.

(iii) The Engine House (now the Students Union), with the tall fortress-like **Water Tower** adjoining. Both structures are of 1890, and are linked to the Mansion by a covered arcade.

(iv) The western part of the Mansion. The tall block on the right, with its glazed attic storey, is the old Picture Gallery of 1890, now the Library, though the red brick section facing north is an extension of 1910. The single storey section to its left is the old Sculpture Gallery of 1890, now also part of the Library.

(v) The large porte-cochere of the 1890 building. Note the fine stone carving over and around the entrance, embracing the date 1890, and the ironwork in the windows.

(vi) The eastern part of the Mansion, including the admin block c1963, and the Norbert Singer Lecture Theatre of 1996.

(vii) **Bird Sanctuary Building**, with TV studio and arts studio, adjoining to the west, of the late 1960s.

(viii) The Tower Block, including media resources and computer suite, of 1971.

The *interior, with its lavish and extravagant decorative work, is well worth viewing. The most interesting rooms are the surviving rooms of the 1890 building, particularly the Sculpture Gallery and the Picture Gallery; and there is a small room (the Boyd Room) surviving from the previous house of c1841 on the site. These rooms all now form part of the Library.

The interior is not generally open to the public; however, it is worth asking at Reception (or phoning 020-8850 4253 in advance) for permission to look around.

The entrance porch (note the carved mahogany doors) leads into the large **Entrance Hall**, with a glazed dome above; on the left is an elaborate carved marble chimneypiece, with classical figures and pre-Raphaelite style tiles, and there are some finely carved wooden panels.

A corridor leading out of the right-hand part of the Entrance Hall leads to the **Senior Common Room**, which was the original drawing room. Before entering note the inlaid ivory doors, and the busts of John North and his wife on either side. The room preserves the original round arched windows and doors, some of which had direct access to the Winter Garden.

The **Library** opens out directly to the right of the Entrance Hall; it occupies several old rooms - Sculpture Gallery, Boyd Room, Picture Gallery, Garden Court. First you enter the **Sculpture Gallery**, with its marble walls, pilasters and floor. Immediately to the left is the **Boyd Room** c1841, a perfect cube, though the arched recesses were added when North made it his library. At the end of the Sculpture Gallery is the vast **Picture Gallery**, or Great Hall, with a green marble doorcase, and a screen of 16 green onyx pillars, which support a minstrels gallery and separate the Hall from a former conservatory. The coving beneath the clerestory was brilliantly restored in 1994 with the original intricate decorative pattern; it is best viewed by ascending the spiral staircase to the balcony. Leading off the Picture Gallery near the entrance is the **Garden Court**, once a totally enclosed small conservatory.

In the eastern part of the Mansion the only surviving room from the old building is the Ladies Cloakroom, with ornately tiled walls and ceiling, and stained glass windows.

A road from the gateway leads behind the Mansion to the ***Winter Garden (52C)**, constructed c1890 and originally directly accessible from the house through the present Senior Common Room. Note the statue of Mercury on top.

It is a magnificent conservatory consisting of: a temperate house with a dome about 30 metres high, and palms, citrus, cacti and other succulents, orchids, philodendron, bougainvillea, strelitzia regina etc all around; a tropical house with ferns, anthurium, bananas, bromeliads etc; and a cool house with camelias, acacias etc. In the cool house a large goldfish-pond has a luscious statue of the Greek goddess Galatea reclining on a dolphin, by Leopoldo Ansiglioni 1880.

The Winter Garden is open daily 1000-1600, except at lunchtime; closed first Monday in the month, and on Xmas Day, Boxing Day, New Years Day.

To the west of the Winter Garden is a large walled garden, including rose and flower gardens. Further west, beyond the access road, are the **stud groom's cottage** and **stables (52D)**, mostly sited around a courtyard, of John North's stud farm of 1890.

To the south of the Mansion is **Avery Hill Park (52E)**, a large public park. To the west of the park, stretching as far as the LESSA pond *(see 40A)* and Footscray Road, is **Avery Hill Fields**, a vast network of sports grounds and playing fields, separated by belts of trees and hedgerows, linked by a network of paths. Some of the hedgerows are quite ancient, and the whole area is very natural. The River Shuttle, originating in Pippenhall Meadows *(see 51)*, flows as a narrow stream through the fields.

The view of the buildings from the Park is dominated by the dome of the Winter Garden and the roof of the Picture Gallery at the west end, and theTower Block at the east end. Note the series of classical round arched windows, which go round the Senior Common Room, the Winter Garden, and the former conservatory at the end of the Picture Gallery. Outside the Winter Garden is a row of tall eucalyptus trees.

157 Bexley Road (52F), a large red brick building to the north of the campus at the corner of Riefield Road, is the old farmhouse c1890 of John North's Model Farm.

Beyond the park, and accessible from Avery Hill Road, are a group of hostels and other college buildings, centred on ***Southwood House (52G)**. This fine house, facing south, is late 18th century, though stuccoed later and with substantial later extensions. North lived here during the construction of Avery Hill Mansion. It was

purchased by the London County Council in 1908 as a hostel for students at Avery Hill. Adjacent is the mid 19th century **Southwood Lodge**.
To the west are three great grey four-storey hostel blocks of 1913-16. Beyond is the **Southwood Site**, or student residential village, of the University of Greenwich, built 1994-96. The campus consists mainly of rather utilitarian brick blocks, but it is quite pleasant around the student union building called 'The Dome'. In a lily-pond near the Dome is **The Witch of Agnesi**, a strange sculpture by F.E. McWilliam 1959. (Agnesi was a medieval woman mathematician, considered at the time to be a witch.)
Outside the entrance to Southwood House, on a small green at the junction of Avery Hill Road and Halfway Street, is a **finger signpost** *(see also New Eltham 5)*.
Southwood Cottages (52H), 201/209 Avery Hill Road, is a pleasing late 19th century terrace built for gardeners on the Southwood House estate. Alongside, set back, is **199 Avery Hill Road**, an imposing house with a loggia, converted c1908 from a former estate building of c1860.

53. *Environmental Curriculum Centre, Bexley Road. This is a wonderful place, a nature reserve which serves as an educational resource for schools. It was originally the ILEA Nature Study Scheme, and occupies harmonious functional buildings of 1960; since 1990 it has been operated by the London Borough of Greenwich.
The site is large, and incorporates an amazing variety of wildlife habitats, including meadows of wild flowers, cornfields, hedgerows, woodlands. There are two ponds fed by a tributary of the River Shuttle, as well as artificial ponds.
As the site is intended for schools, there is no access for the general public. However, open days are held from time to time, and such is the appeal of the site, it is worth phoning 020-8850 2615 to check whether it is possible to visit.

54. *Gravel Pit Lane. This winding footpath, part of the Green Chain Walk, is an ancient country lane; though mostly broad and well surfaced, it remains delightfully rural, flanked by trees and shrubs. Extensive gravel extraction took place here in the mid 18th century. It passes between Eltham Warren Golf Course on one side (note the small pond), and Crown Woods School and the Environmental Curriculum Centre *(see 53)* on the other. There is a horse trough of 1905 at the Bexley Road end.

55. Crown Woods School, Riefield Road. A large, sprawling complex; the central part is of 1954, in a subdued modernist style with mainly glass curtain walling.

56. Eltham Cemetery has a formal layout of 1935; there are some fine old oak trees, but otherwise there is no landscape interest. The main buildings are: a red brick Gothic chapel of 1935, with an octagonal tower; the Crematorium of 1956, with a tall square tower, with another chapel added in 1975; and the Chapel of Remembrance, c1966, modern and circular, with a vertical pattern of full height projecting stone sections alternating with full height recessed glazed sections, which are seen on the interior as stained glass in modern geometric design. Behind this Chapel is the Flower Pavilion, and in front the Memorial Courts of 1996, both attractive additions. In the west section there is a prominent monument to Ernest Bennett, a young airman who died in a flying accident in 1938; the figure is dressed in an airman's uniform.

57. Falconwood Station. A railway station of 1936 on the Bexleyheath Line, which had been laid down in 1895. In art deco style, it was opened to serve the newly built Falconwood Park Estate of New Ideal Homesteads in Welling.

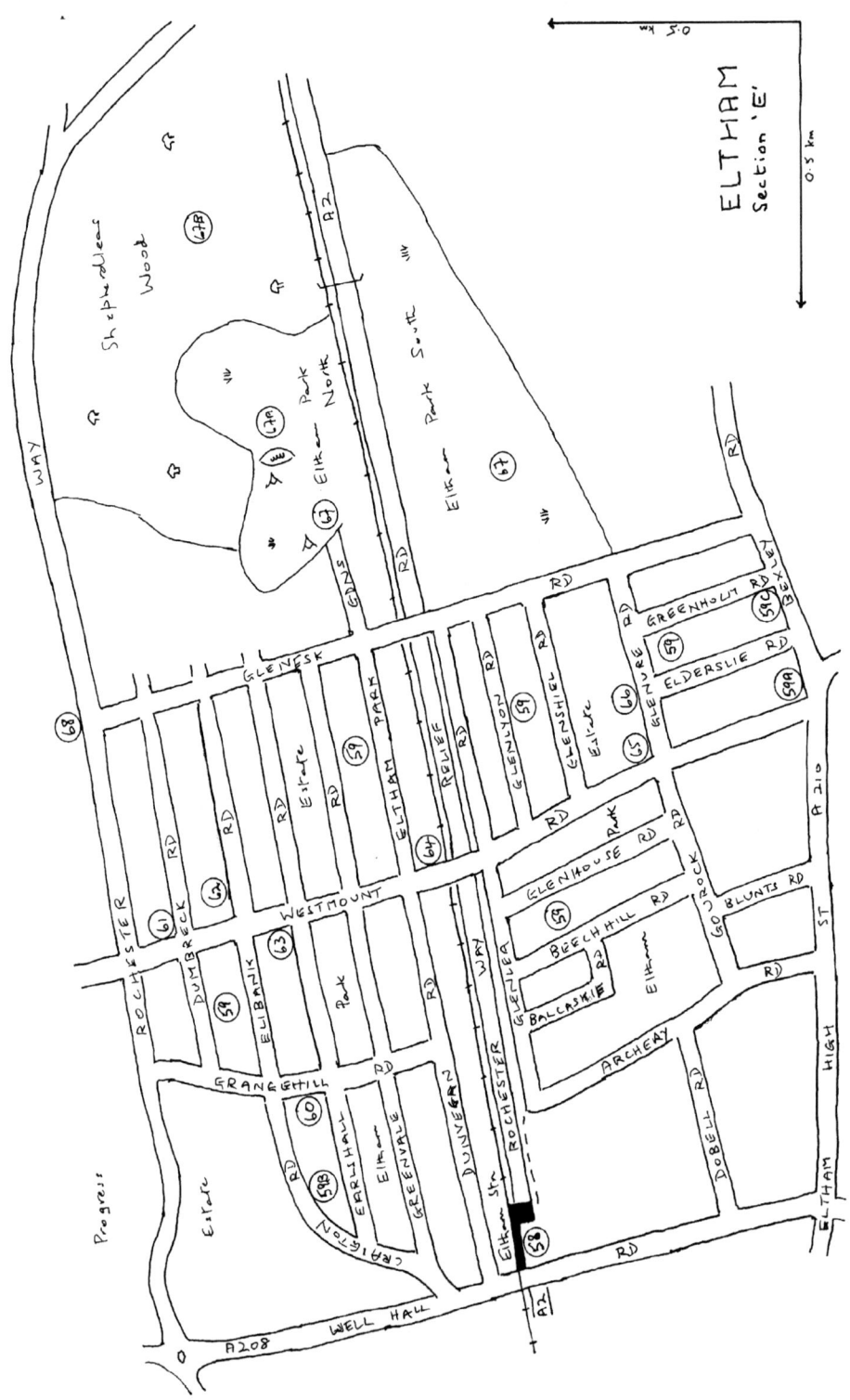

ELTHAM

Gazetteer

Section 'E' ELTHAM PARK

58. Eltham Station. A spacious modern station on the Bexleyheath Line, with a bus station in the forecourt outside. The dominant features of the complex are the red metalwork, and the glazed upper level where the 'up' platform is located.

> The railway station was built in 1985 to replace Eltham Well Hall and Eltham Park; both stations were closed in connection with the construction of the Rochester Way Relief Road, which goes in a tunnel under the forecourt of the new station. Eltham Well Hall was opened in 1895 as Well Hall Station, and was renamed Well Hall & North Eltham in 1916, and Eltham Well Hall in 1927. It was on the opposite side of the road from the new station, but has been demolished completely. Of Eltham Park Station, however, some traces do remain *(see 64)*.

59. *Eltham Park Estate. A large estate, developed by Cameron Corbett and built between 1900 and 1914.

> Cameron Corbett, later Lord Rowallan, was a major Edwardian developer in the London area. Besides Eltham Park, his other major estates are at Hither Green, Ilford and Forest Gate.

The pivotal road is Westmount Road, with the railway station originally built for the estate (now closed - *see 64)*, a shopping centre, and the churches. Some roads have much modern infill.

The houses are of red brick, mostly with stone dressings; they are well designed and solidly built, and are predominantly in long terraces, which can become monotonous. But any monotony is often offset by variety in size and detailing, and the overall effect is mostly quite attractive. Note in particular the following:

(i) **Craigton Road** and the western parts of **Earlshall Road** and **Greenvale Road**, the first area to be developed, c1900-03 - there are prominent door and window surrounds, and in most cases alternating male and female mask keystones over the doorways.

(ii) the southern part of **Westmount Road**, built c1900-03 - the larger double-fronted houses without any stone dressings at all are perhaps the most stately, some with terracotta patterns over the doorways.

(iii) **Greenholm Road**, built c1900-03 - the regular pattern of door and window surrounds, and the dentilled pediments and other ornamental embellishments, make this a particularly handsome street.

(iv) **Gourock Road** and **Glenhouse Road**, built c1905-08 - a number of houses have bargeboards, dentilled pediments and other ornamental flourishes.

(v) **Beechhill Road** and **Balcaskie Road**, built c1905-08 - strong gables over substantial bays, with a powerful sequence of stone dressings.

(vi) **Dunvegan Road** and **Eltham Park Gardens**, built c1908-11 - prominent gables over substantial projecting polygonal bays.

(vii) **Glenshiel Road** and **Glenlyon Road**, built c1908-11 - powerful pairs with positive polygonal bays at each end flanking recessed entrance bays.

(viii) **Glenesk Road**, built c1908-11 - there are a number of imposing double-fronted houses with bold half-timbered gables.

(ix) **251/279 Eltham High Street (59A)**, built c1900-03 - this parade of shops forms a slightly skewed terrace, looking particularly elegant along the upper floors above the modern shopfronts.

44 Craigton Road (59B) has a small plaque erected in association with the British Film Institute 1996: 'Bob Hope, actor & entertainer, born here 29th May 1903'.

A total contrast, on the fringe of the estate, is provided by **1a Greenholm Road (59C)**, by Edward Cullinan 1966. It occupies a long narrow site, and is difficult to see from the road. Note the largely glazed upper floor, the sheer brick wall to the south, and the very steeply pitched roof.

60. Gordon School. A large and imposing school in brick and terracotta, designed by Thomas Bailey for the London School Board 1904. The frontage towards Grangehill Road is quite baroque. A powerful frontispiece consists of rusticated terracotta pilasters flanking full height double arches, with rows of bulbous columns in the top gable and on the ground floor. Note also the circular windows, surrounded by swirling stone carving, in gables on both frontages.

61. Church of St Luke, Westmount Road. A simple Gothic red brick church designed by Temple Moore 1907; the south aisle was an incongruous addition of 1933. The interior *(contact the Vicarage, 107 Westmount Road, or phone 020-8850 3030)* is lofty, with an imposing wagon roof. There are two wide arcade arches to the north aisle, and three narrower arches to the south aisle.

62. Eltham Park Chapel, Elibank Road, was originally Eltham Park Gospel Hall of 1913, enlarged 1959. Within the full-width gable is a Gothic window, and there are Gothic windows on both sides of the Tudor entrance.

63. Eltham Park Methodist Church, Westmount Road, a strange red brick church of 1906 with Gothic and Tudor motifs. The entrance has a bold and wide traceried Gothic window flanked by pinnacles. There are two rows of Tudor windows along each side. To the right at the end of the courtyard is a church room with Gothic windows, contemporary with the church. A new church hall and the residential John Wesley Court were added in 1989.

It is worth trying to view the **interior** *(contact 020-8850 2406)*. The chancel was formerly apsed, but the apse was blocked in 1968 (though on the exterior it is still visible from Earlshall Road). The striking cantilevered gallery is original, though considerably extended in 1990. In the vestibule is the original foundation stone, inscribed 'Wesleyan Chapel 1840', of Eltham's first Methodist chapel, which was in Elizabeth Terrace.

64. Eltham Park Station (remains). The station was originally built to a design of Alfred Blomfield in 1908 to serve the Eltham Park Estate, already at that time well advanced in construction. It was quite splendid, with covered walkways down ramps to the canopied platforms.

On the Bexleyheath Line, it was originally called Shooters Hill & Eltham Park Station, and was renamed Eltham Park in 1927. It was closed in 1985 and replaced by Eltham Station *(see 58)*.

The remains (which can be viewed from Glenlea Road across the Rochester Way Relief Road) consist of the platforms and, behind the shops, a short and derelict section of the wooden covered walkway.

The original station building is now **92/98 Westmount Road**, having in 1922 become a parade of shops; no 96 with its distinctive upper part was the original entrance and booking office.

65. Eltham Park Baptist Church, Westmount Road. A large stock brick Gothic church of 1912. The main entrance, facing south, has a large Gothic window with swirling tracery above, and there are similar Gothic windows to the north and (though smaller) along both sides. The hall to the right was rebuilt 1958, and is now linked to the church by the Friendship Centre of 1997.

It is worth asking for permission to view the **interior** *(call at the Friendship Centre, or phone 020-8859 7740)*. It is spacious and imposing, with a fine timber roof and a south gallery. Ask to see the original chapel of 1903 at the rear, though it is much altered; it is not visible from the road.

66. St Mary's School, Glenure Road. The long white building to the left was built c1912 for St Clotilde Convent School; the school hall, the red brick building set back to the right, was added in the interwar period. Note on the original building the central classical porch, now blocked. On the left side is the present entrance, a portico of four classical columns which is probably a survivor from a mid 19th century rebuild of Eltham Park House, the previous building on the site.

> Eltham Park House, originally known as Park Farm Place, was built 1774 by Sir William James, a commander in the East India Company. After his death his widow in 1784 built Severndroog Castle in Castle Wood to celebrate his naval exploits *(see Shooters Hill 8, also Eltham 20A)*. Eltham Park House was largely rebuilt in the mid 19th century.
>
> The mansion was sold to Cameron Corbett in 1900, and was acquired by the Roman Catholic Church in 1901. St Clotilde Convent School, run by a French order, moved there in 1910, demolished the mansion (probably leaving the portico), built a new school c1912 and stayed on the site until 1938. After the war, it became Ave Maria Community School until 1984, when St Mary's School moved here; it had previously occupied St Mary's Centre in the High Street *(see 30)*, and other buildings nearby which were then demolished for the Sainsbury development.

Between the school and the Baptist Church is **St Josephs Cottage**, a white house c1905 with deep eaves, which had been a lodge for St Clotilde School.

Behind the school to the right is the **Bethlehem House of Prayer (Convent of Mercy)**, occupying a mainly postwar building, and **Coniffe Court**, a post-modern housing development of 1989.

67. Eltham Park. This large area of open space is divided by the railway line and the Rochester Way Relief Road, which run alongside each other in a deep cutting (there is a good view of the road and the railway running through the park from the bridge in Glenesk Road). On one side is Eltham Park South (acquired by the London County Council in 1903), and on the other Eltham Park North (acquired by the LCC in 1929), which also embraces Shepherdleas Wood (acquired 1934).

Eltham Park South consists of a large grassed area with sports facilities.

*****Eltham Park North**, with its woodlands, has a special atmosphere, particularly around the **Long Pond (67A).** This is an ancient pond, highly attractive with its overhanging trees, small island and water birds; Shepherdleas Wood looms nearby and there are fine views to the west towards Crystal Palace, Sydenham Hill and Honor Oak, with the taller buildings of Central London visible in the distance. There are similar views nearer the entrance in Eltham Park Gardens.

*****Shepherdleas Wood (67B)** was acquired by the LCC at the same time as Oxleas Wood *(see Shooters Hill 11)* on the other side of Rochester Way, which had been driven through the woodlands by 1930. It has similar characteristics to Oxleas Wood; it is designated a Site of Special Scientific Interest, and is classified as ancient woodland, though there have been many planted trees. The dominant tree is the oak, and there are also numbers of sweet chestnut, hawthorn, aspen, hazel, birch, ash, wild cherry, as well as the rarer wild service tree, of which there are many specimens at the western edge and at one point in the centre. There is also a wide variety of shrubs, herbs and other plants in dense undergrowth; there is a fine display of bluebells in the late spring, particularly on the western side of the site.

68. Deansfield School, an attractive complex consisting of three separate main buildings in classical style, built for the London County Council 1903-06. Note the fine gables, many with elegant oval or circular windows, dentilled cornices, and other classical features. The school bears some similarities to Timbercroft School, Plumstead.

ELTHAM

Gazetteer

Section 'F' WELL HALL
(See map on page 48)

69. **Well Hall. An attractive and fascinating building (now called the Tudor Barn), as well as moat walls, a bridge, and some garden walls have survived from the grounds of the Tudor mansion of Well Hall; all are now set within a pleasant park.

> The estate of Well Hall goes back at least to the 13th century. In the early 16th century a mansion called Well Hall was built by the Roper family on the moated site of an earlier house, and some medieval structure may have been retained. A member of the family, William Roper, married Sir Thomas More's daughter Margaret in 1521.
>
> In 1733 the estate was purchased by Sir Gregory Page, to add to his already extensive Wricklemarsh estate at Blackheath. He demolished the Tudor house and built a large new mansion on the other side of the moat to the east.
>
> From 1779 to 1799 this mansion, also called Well Hall, was occupied by John Arnold, who competed (unsuccessfully) with John Harrison to invent the first chronometer to keep perfect time at sea; however, he went on to create an accurate but simplified chronometer which he was then able to mass produce.
>
> From 1899 to 1922 the house was occupied by the children's writer Edith Nesbit and her husband Hubert Bland, a founder of the Fabian Society. Her famous book 'The Railway Children' was written here. The house and the bell, now fixed to the outside of the Tudor Barn, are mentioned in Edith Nesbit's books.
>
> The house was badly damaged by fire in 1926, and the whole site was acquired by the then Metropolitan Borough of Woolwich in 1929 to become Well Hall Pleasaunce. The house was demolished in 1931, and a surviving Tudor building, known as the Tudor Barn, was in 1936 converted to an art gallery on the upper floor and a restaurant on the ground floor. The building has been a pub, using both floors, since 1995.

Nothing remains of the 16th century Tudor mansion within the moated area. But the ***moat (69A)** with its largely Tudor brick banks, and the Tudor stone-arched ***bridge** to the east have survived. There is a modern wooden bridge over the moat to the west.

The Tudor Barn and the Well Hall site are set within an attractive park, **Well Hall Pleasaunce (69B)**, noted for its displays of spring bulbs. Substantial sections of the original Tudor garden walls to the south have been preserved; in the westernmost walls five triangular-headed niches (some blocked), which may have been bee-boles, can be seen. The park is about to be restored.

The ****Tudor Barn (69C)**, now a pub, was part of the original Tudor complex of buildings; its original purpose is unknown, but it was probably not a barn. It is a well preserved red brick building, facing the site of the main mansion across the north arm of the moat; an extension to the moat runs along the west side of the building. A coat of arms on the north front bears the date 1568, but it is generally considered to date from earlier in the 16th century.

Original features include the patterned black brick, the chimneystacks at the west end, and the rectangular mullioned windows (some blocked) at the east end; the

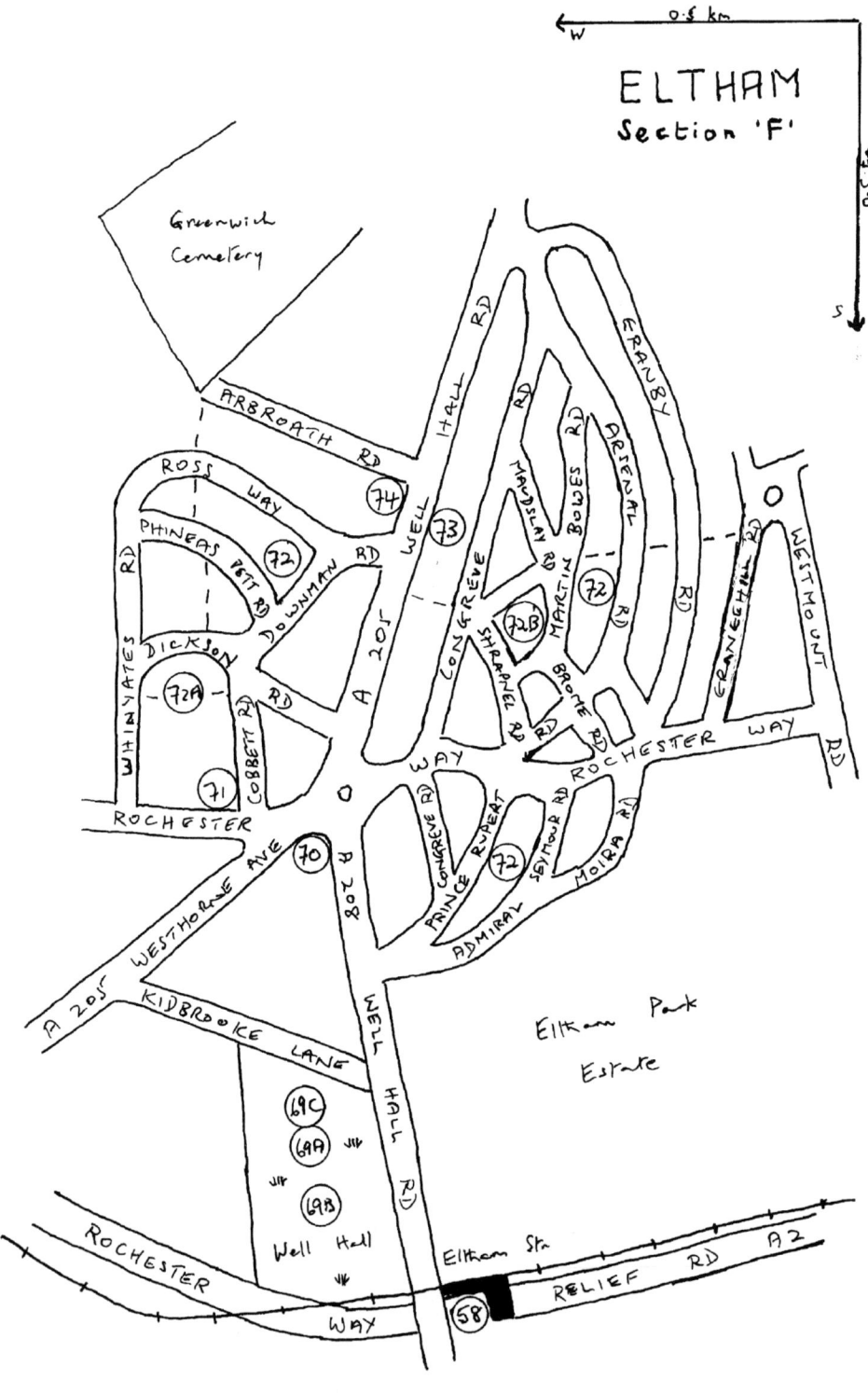

windows at the west end are 17th century. On the east wall the monogram WR (William Roper) and Edith Nesbit's bell can be seen.

The white column by the lawn facing the entrance is a sundial of 1941.

The *interior is worth viewing, especially for the Tudor fireplaces on both floors.
Access to the ground floor presents no problems during pub opening hours. Ask at the bar about access to the upper floor, which is normally permitted unless there is a function taking place.
On the ground floor, note at the west end an original Tudor brick fireplace, and a section of distinctive stone and pebble tiled flooring (which was imported later).

The upper floor is dominated by the exposed roof timbers. Note at the west end an original Tudor red brick fireplace, and on the south wall a later Tudor stone fireplace with fine carving. In the west wall is a small stained glass window showing Thomas More and his daughter Margaret Roper, designed after Holbein's portrait by Margaret Cowell 1949.

70. Former Coronet Cinema, Well Hall Road. This former Odeon cinema of 1936, designed by Andrew Mather, has some interesting art deco features - note the projecting glass staircase tower, and the circular canopy over the entrance. The interior of the foyer is also circular, with a circular wooden ticket booth and the word Odeon in green and red mosaic set into the floor. Unfortunately, the cinema has recently closed, and it may be difficult to find a future use for the building.

71. Church of St Barnabas, Rochester Way. A Victorian Gothic church in red brick, designed by Sir George Gilbert Scott. It was originally built in 1859 as the chapel of the Royal Naval Dockyard at Woolwich; it was dismantled and re-erected, brick by brick, on this site in 1933. The exterior is rather stark, with a bold apse, quirky turret and many lancet windows; along the side are four gables, each covering twin lancets.

The **interior** *(contact the vicarage next door, or ring 020-8856 8294, 8850 3547)* was transformed by Thomas Ford in 1957 after war damage. It is light and spacious, with a wagon roof and a large flowing mural by Hans Feibusch on the apse ceiling; but it is very strange ('sickly Regency wedding-cake' - Pevsner), with 16 angels perched on beams above columns in the square arcades. Note the anthemium motifs in the arcades. The Stations of the Cross are of some interest, by Stan Boundy c1994.

The vicarage next door is a striking red brick house c1955, with a graceful ground floor bow. Adjacent is the church hall, of 1938, renamed Frankie Howerd Community Centre in 1988.

72. **Progress Estate. A remarkable 'garden suburb' estate of nearly 1300 houses built in 1915, the principal architect being Sir Frank Baines.

> The estate was a government development to house workers at the Royal Arsenal during the First World War, and was completed in only 11 months. Originally known as the Well Hall Estate, it was renamed Progress Estate when purchased by the Royal Arsenal Co-operative Society in 1925. The houses are now mostly privately owned, though some are owned by a housing association.

It was built straddling Well Hall Road, with a large area to the east of the road, and a smaller area to the west. In 1930 Rochester Way was constructed through the larger area, thus slicing it in two.

The estate with its greens, trees, curving roads and footpaths, and an amazing variety of house styles, has an essentially village atmosphere, very picturesque in places. Even the main roads manage to preserve this appeal - Well Hall Road with some particularly attractive frontages, and Rochester Way with its winding route.

The housing groups are often skilfully designed, with contrasting styles and an imaginatively informal (sometimes almost crazily irregular) layout providing constant surprise as one walks around. Some groups are set quite near a road or a green, others are set well back. Winding roads reveal delightful perspectives and road junctions provide enclosed views.

There are a number of recurring features which contribute to the atmosphere, like footpaths passing under houses, steep-pitched roofs with dormers, mansard roofs, large chimney-stacks, dominant gables, overhanging first floors (some supported on pillars), large bays projecting towards the road, rectangular mullioned windows. There is a variety of surfaces - brick, slate-hung, tile-hung, weatherboarded, half-timbered, stuccoed, whitewashed, pebbledash, roughcast.

It is difficult to single out particular streets and groups, but the following in each of the three parts are particularly worth viewing:

(a) West of Well Hall Road (the most appealing area). **Ross Way**, sinuously curving, with its raised pavement; **Whinyates Road**, and its delightful junction with Dickson Road; **Sandby Green (72A)**, an enclosed and intimate green, with a footpath leading under a house into Whinyates Road; the footpath leading from Arbroath Road downhill via Ross Way to Phineas Pett Road, and thence down by Franklin Passage to Dickson Road; the bow-shaped **Phineas Pett Road**; the picturesque groups on either side of the junction of Downman Road with Well Hall Road.

(b) East of Well Hall Road, north of Rochester Way. **Lovelace Green (72B)**, a large village green with a real village atmosphere, fringed by attractive houses; the footpath leading from Lovelace Green through an X-shaped group and emerging under a half-timbered upper floor into Well Hall Road; the semi-circular terrace facing a green on Well Hall Road; the bow-shaped **Arsenal Road**.

(c) East of Well Hall Road, south of Rochester Way. **Prince Rupert Road**, and the junction with Admiral Seymour Road; the semi-circular terrace facing a green on Well Hall Road.

73. Set into the pavement on the east side of Well Hall Road, almost opposite the Martyrs Church, is the **memorial plaque to Stephen Lawrence**, victim of a racist murder on this spot at the age of 18 years in 1993: 'In memory of Stephen Lawrence, 1974 - 1993, may he rest in peace'.

74. The Martyrs Church, Well Hall Road. A Roman Catholic church, dedicated to St John Fisher and St Thomas More. This brick church, designed by O'Hanlon Hughes 1936, does not have much impact from the road; its rectangular box-like shape, with tall lancet windows, is offset by two towers set diagonally at the east end.

But the *interior is of great interest *(contact the Presbytery behind the church, or phone 020-8856 4993)*. It is modern and functional, and embodies two structural features considered pioneering at the time - the aisle roofs are unsupported by pillars, and the main lighting is by a series of circular windows in the nave and aisle roofs. The orientation is to the west. On either side of the sanctuary are strange stylised stone statues in bas-relief of the two martyrs by Lindsay Clarke. In a small chapel off the north aisle is a vivid stained glass window by David Whalley 1988.

ELTHAM

Suggested Walks

It is recommended that the five suggested walks be followed in conjunction with the Gazetteer and the maps, and that the Gazetteer be consulted at each location for a detailed description. Some locations described in the Gazetteer have not been included, as they might add too much to the length of the walks.
Walk no 1 covers Section 'B', Walk no 2 Section 'C', Walk no 3 Section 'D', Walk no 4 Section 'E', and Walk no 5 Section 'F'. Section 'A' is not covered, as Eltham Palace needs a separate visit and the gazetteer entry indicates a suggested route, which includes the Great Hall, Courtauld House, and the grounds.
The walks follow a more or less circular route, so can be joined at any location. They begin and end at Eltham Station, except Walk no 3 which is an extension of Walk no 2.

WALK No 1 (including the exterior of Eltham Palace, King John's Walk, Middle Park Estate, Eltham Lodge, Court Road). Distance approx five kilometres (approx three kilometres if begun and ended at the Church of St John the Baptist).

NB. It is worth trying to make an advance arrangement - see the gazetteer - to view the interior of St Saviours Church. Bear in mind that sections of King John's Walk can at times become quite muddy.

On leaving **Eltham Station (58)** turn left and walk up Well Hall Road as far as the crossroads, with the **Church of St John the Baptist (20)** on the right. Cross Eltham High Street and walk down Court Yard until the road bears slightly left to become Court Road; at this point go straight ahead along the continuation of **Court Yard (3)**. Note the old walls of **Chaundrye Close (3A)** on the right.

At the junction turn left into **Tilt Yard Approach (4)** to see the Tudor gateway and wall, then return to Court Yard, noting **The Gatehouse (3B)** on the corner. Continue along Court Yard, noting the old walls on both sides, and to the right **nos 32/32a** and nos 34/38, the **Lord Chancellor's Lodgings (2)**.

At the end of Court Yard is the entrance to **Eltham Palace (1)**, with the **moat bridge** and the north moat wall, and across the moat a view of the front of **Courtauld House** and the **Great Hall**. Bear right down **King John's Walk (5)** and on reaching **nos 1/3 (5A)**, turn sharp left. Continue downhill along King John's Walk until you reach Middle Park Avenue, on the **Middle Park Estate (6)**. Turn right along Middle Park Avenue until you reach the **Church of St Saviour (7)**; try to see the interior. If you have time, continue along Middle Park Avenue for half a kilometre to **Eltham Green (9)**, then retrace steps.

From St Saviours Church, go back along Middle Park Avenue until you come to the junction with Court Road; **Mottingham Station** is to the right, and **The Tarn (14)** opposite.

Walk round the lake in The Tarn; on leaving The Tarn, turn right along **Court Road (15)**, noting the houses on both sides. On reaching the driveway to the Royal

Blackheath Golf Club on the right, walk along to **Eltham Lodge (16)** and ask permission to look at the exterior *(see page 27)*. Return to Court Road and turn right, and continue along Court Road (again noting the houses on both sides) and Court Yard to the crossroads. Cross to Well Hall Road and back to Eltham Station.

WALK No 2 (including St Johns Church, Eltham High Street, Southend, Philipot Path and Eltham Hill). Distance approx four kilometres.

Try to make advance arrangements - see the gazetteer - to see the interiors of St Johns Church and Holy Trinity Church.

On leaving **Eltham Station (58)** turn left and walk up Well Hall Road as far as the crossroads. The **Church of St John the Baptist (20)** is on the right; try to see the interior, and also look at the **burial ground (20A)**. On leaving the churchyard by the lych-gate, note the buildings at the **crossroads (21)**, then cross into Eltham High Street, walking along the south side.

Passing **The Greyhound (22)** and **Mellins (23)**, you then reach **Passey Place (24)**; turn right to look at **The Old Post Office** and **The Park Tavern**, then return. Look at **Cliefden (25)** opposite, then cross the road, go down the lane alongside no 105 to see the rear of Cliefden and the old **stables**. Continue along the lane until you come to **The Orangery (26)**, now awaiting restoration. Retrace steps and and turn left along the north side of the High Street.

On reaching **Barclays Bank (27)**, go through the gateway to see **no 131b** behind. Continue along the High Street, noting **no 130, nos 132/136** and **nos 146/150 (28)** opposite. Look down the cul-de-sac of Roper Street to see **Eltham Church of England School (29)**. Note **St Marys Centre (30)** on the opposite side, then cross Archery Road.

Cross to the south side of the High Street. Note the group formed by **Eltham Library**, the **Eletriq Cafe** and **The Rising Sun (32)** opposite, then look at **The Arcade (33)**. Cross the High Street again to the north side and continue to Blunts Road. Turn left and almost immediately you come to **nos 3/7 (34A)**; opposite is **Fifteenpenny Fields (34)**, which is difficult to see behind Thurland House.

Return to the High Street; note **Eltham Fire Station (35)** opposite. Continue along the north side to **Christ Church Presbytery (36)**, flanked by **Christ Church** and the Priory. Continue past the reservoir and cross Westmount Road.

Cross to **2/14 Southend Crescent (37)**. At this point you can, if you have time, take Walk no 3 to Avery Hill *(see below)*. If not, continue down Southend Crescent, noting houses to the right. Just before **Holy Trinity Church (39)**, take the footpath to the **Conduit Head (38)**, then return to the church; try to see the interior.

Continue down Southend Crescent, noting houses on the opposite side, and bear left along Footscray Road. Walk along the driveway to the London Electricity sports ground to see the **pond (40A)**, then continue to **Southend House (40)**, with the **milestone** outside. Cross the road to **144 Footscray Road (41)**, then turn right and continue along the west side of Footscray Road, noting **nos 48/60 (42)** on the left and **no 59 (43)** on the right. Turn left into Messeter Place.

Take the first road to the right, Elm Terrace, and turn left along the footway which passes the end of The Arcade; this is the beginning of **Philipot Path (44)**. The path continues through a shopping precinct, and beyond begins to have some atmosphere. Note **nos 1/2** and **no 4**, continue and bear left around the **Thomas Philipot**

Almshouse (44A), then bear right and cross Passey Place, with **Eltham & Mottingham House (24A)** on your left.

Continue along Philipot Path, and after **nos 23/24**, turn right into **Elizabeth Terrace (45)**, passing between the cottages and their front gardens; retrace steps back to Philipot Path and continue to the road junction.

Cross the road into Wythfield Road, then bear right, passing the **Bob Hope Theatre (46)**, until you reach Eltham High Street. **The Chequers (47)** and its **milestone** are immediately on the right. Turn left down Eltham High Street, which soon becomes Eltham Hill. Pass no 150, **Queenscroft (48)**, and a section of **reconstructed wall** of the Eltham Palace grounds (3) (with a plaque by the Eltham Society), then cross Kingsground to **Mecca Bingo (49)** and **Eltham Hill School (50)**, with its Tudor **garden house**.

Cross Eltham Hill and turn right, then turn left into Sherard Road and continue until you are back at Eltham Station.

WALK No 3 (including Avery Hill, Pippenhall Meadows and Gravel Pit Lane). This walk is an extension to Walk no 2; it begins and ends at the junction of Eltham High Street and Southend Crescent. Distance approx two and a half kilometres.

Try to make advance arrangements - see the gazetteer - to see the interior of Avery Hill. The Winter Garden is closed for one hour at lunchtime, and on the first Monday in the month.

Beyond Southend Crescent, Eltham High Street becomes Bexley Road; proceed along Bexley Road on the south side. Pass the riding stables and a public field, which are part of **Pippenhall Meadows (51)**, then just before the allotments and near the **milestone**, take the footpath to the right, which runs alongside old hedgerows. Follow the footpath for some distance, then retrace steps to Bexley Road and turn right.

You quickly arrive at **Avery Hill (52)**. From the **gatehouse (52A)** follow the driveway to the entrance of the **Mansion (52B)**; ask permission to see the interior. Return and take the access road to the left just before the gatehouse, which leads round to the **Winter Garden (52C)**. Return to the gatehouse and turn right along Bexley Road. Follow the wall, then cross at the traffic lights into Riefield Road. Note the old farmhouse at **157 Bexley Road (52F)** on the opposite corner.

Continue up Riefield Road, and after passing **Crown Woods School (55)**, turn left along a path between fences which opens out into **Gravel Pit Lane (54)**. The footpath passes between Eltham Warren Golf Course on the right, and the grounds of Crown Woods School and the **Environmental Curriculum Centre (53)** on the left. At the junction with Bexley Road, turn right. Continue along Bexley Road until you are back at **Southend Crescent (37)**, where you can rejoin Walk no 2.

WALK No 4 (including the Corbett Estate and Eltham Park). Distance approx four kilometres.

Try to make advance arrangements - see the gazetteer - to view the interiors of St Lukes Church and the Methodist Church. The visit to Eltham Park can be extended by a walk through Shepherdleas Wood, but bear in mind that the paths can become quite muddy.

On leaving **Eltham Station (58)** turn right along Well Hall Road. Take the second road on the right, **Craigton Road**, which leads into the **Eltham Park Estate (59)**. Bear left along Craigton Road, noting **no 44 (59B)** and continue to Grangehill Road.

Turn right, passing **Gordon School (60)**, then take the first road on the left, Earlshall Road, as far as Westmount Road.
Turn left, passing **Eltham Park Methodist Church (63)**; try to see the interior. Continue to the **Church of St Luke (61)** on the right; try to see the interior. Retrace steps along Westmount Road and continue to **nos 92/98**, the old building of **Eltham Park Station (64)**, and the bridge over the railway line and Rochester Way Relief Road. Continue along Westmount Road to **Eltham Park Baptist Church (65)**; try to see the interior. Then turn left along Glenure Road, passing **St Josephs Cottage** and **St Mary's School (66)**, and take the second road to the right, **Greenholm Road**, noting **no 1a (59C)** at the end on the right.
Turn left into Bexley Road, and left again into Glenesk Road. Continue past **Eltham Park South** and the bridge over the railway line and Rochester Way Relief Road, then turn right along **Eltham Park Gardens** into **Eltham Park North (67)**, and beyond the staff yard, bear right to the **Long Pond (67A)**. From here, as from nearer the park entrance, there is a fine view over South London and towards Central London, and **Shepherdleas Wood (67B)** looms nearby. Return to Glenesk Road, turn left and turn right along Glenlea Road. Follow the road and then a pathway back to Eltham Station.

WALK No 5 (including Well Hall and Progress Estate). Distance approx three kilometres.

Try to make advance arrangements - see the gazetteer - to view the interior of St Barnabas Church.

On leaving **Eltham Station (58)** turn right along Well Hall Road. Walk under the railway bridge, then cross the road to **Well Hall (69)**. Look at the **Tudor Barn (69C)** (try to see the interior, both floors), the **moat (69A)** and **bridge,** and walk round **Well Hall Pleasaunce (69B)**. Return to Well Hall Road and continue as far as the roundabout, with the **former Coronet Cinema (70)** on the left. Cross Rochester Way, bearing left to the **Church of St Barnabas (71)**; try to see the interior.
Take the road to the right of the church, Cobbett Road, which leads into the **Progress Estate (72)**. Shortly a footpath to the left leads into **Sandby Green (72A)**, and beyond under a house to the junction of Dickson Road with **Whinyates Road**. Follow Whinyates Road and bear right along **Ross Way** to Downman Road, then turn left for Well Hall Road, noting the housing groups at the junction.
Turn left and you immediately come to **The Martyrs Church (74)**; if the church is closed, call at the Presbytery behind and ask for permission to see the interior. Cross the road and note the **memorial plaque to Stephen Lawrence (73)** Bear right, and take the footpath which leads under a house and then across Congreve Road to **Lovelace Green (72B)**. Beyond a smaller green to the left, take the footpath, Cornwallis Walk, which leads into **Arsenal Road**. Turn right and continue down Arsenal Road to Rochester Way. Turn right and follow the winding course of Rochester Way to the roundabout, then turn left along Well Hall Road and back to Eltham Station.

NEW ELTHAM

Gazetteer

(See map on page 56)

1. New Eltham Station. This station in a cutting was opened in 1878 on the Dartford Loop Line, which had been laid down in 1866. Originally called Pope Street Station, it was renamed New Eltham & Pope Street in 1886, and New Eltham in 1927.
   The building on the south (up) side is modern, of 1989, handsome with its fine vaulted station building and vaulted platform canopy.

2. 2/4 Blanmerle Road. A curious and bizarre pair, boldly proclaiming its date of 1898. Chalet-style roofs at crazy angles, and bays set obliquely to the road.

3. The Beehive, 356 Footscray Road. An agreeable pub of 1897, with a large wooden porch. There are lively decorative features, including beehive and sunflower motifs on the porch and in the gables. The interior has fine etched glass.

4. Wyborne School, formerly known as Pope Street School. The smaller building is the original school of 1881. A much larger building, inscribed LSB Pope Street School, was added in 1904 for the London School Board by Thomas Bailey; it is multi-gabled and incorporates an attractive pavilion with a pyramidal roof.

5. Clare Corner. A nice small 'garden suburb' development, on a triangular site at the junction of Footscray Road and Green Lane. It was built by a co-ownership society on land owned by Clare College, Cambridge, in 1914, though some houses were added later. **Cambridge Green** is particularly appealing with its semi-circular housing groups. The residents own a secluded green in the centre, as well as their own tennis court on Cambridge Green.
   Note the white **finger signpost** and horse trough on the green facing the road junction. (There is another finger signpost at the junction of Avery Hill Road and Halfway Street, *see Eltham 52G.*)

6. Victoria Cottages, 84/136 Green Lane. A long and rather picturesque terrace of 1897, forming a gently curved crescent.

7. New Eltham Library, a neo-Georgian building of 1931. Behind is a small park, which leads to Southwood Rough *(see 8B).*

8. Southwood Road has an interesting variety of house styles of many periods, including a number of imposing late 19th century Gothic houses with striking decorative features, built from 1879 after the arrival of the railway.
   Perhaps the most impressive group is on the north side - **nos 86/104 (8A)**, consisting of nos 92/98, two pairs with elegant bargeboards and verandahs, flanked by nos 86/88 and nos 100/104, houses with wide gables, nailhead ornamentation and lots of Gothic windows. Still on the north side, towards the eastern end are some distinctive chalet-style houses of the 1930s.

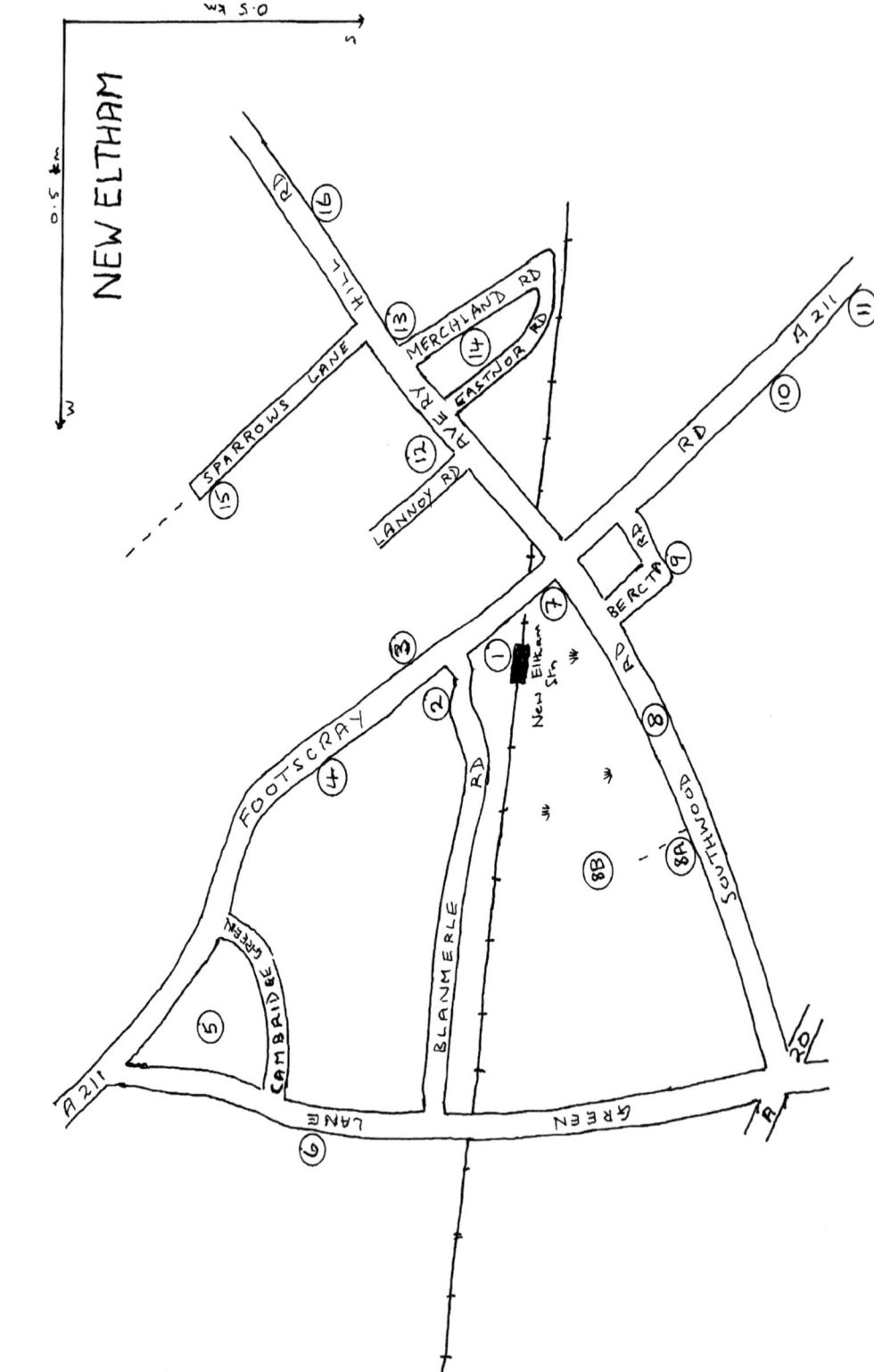

On the south side, note nos 61/75, houses with wide gables and lots of Gothic windows; nos 77/83, two pairs with fine bargeboarded gables; nos 101/103, houses with wide gables over double canted bays; and nos 121/123, with powerful gables.

A path leads from the north side to **Southwood Rough (8B)**, an area of sports fields and allotments fringed by hedgerows, a rural oasis overlooking the railway cutting.

9. All Saints Church, Bercta Road. A basic and, on the exterior, rather uninspired Victorian Gothic red brick church by Peter Dollar of 1898, complicated by the very large chancel added in similar style by Thomas Ford in 1931. The **interior** *(contact the Vicarage next door, or ring 020-8850 9894)* is unexpectedly spacious, with wide arcade arches and a very wide chancel arch. Note the fine stained glass, a tall figure of Christ, in the middle light of the east window, by Caroline Benyon 1999.

Behind the church is **Bishops Close**, a residential development, commenced 1973 and completed 1982, around a pleasant garden square.

10. 468/472 Footscray Road, formerly called **The Grange.** An unusual building c1840, with Tudor arched windows and large Dutch gables over the projecting central bay and at the sides. The section to the right of the central bay was added in the late 1850s in similar style. A tall hedgerow running along the middle of the gardens makes it difficult to appreciate the house as a whole.

11. Outside 494 Footscray Road is a late 18th century **milestone**, erected by the New Cross Turnpike Trust, with early 19th century iron plates reading: '10 miles to London Bridge, 2 miles to Foots Cray'. *See also Eltham 40, 47.*

12. Stanleys, Avery Hill Road. A small industrial estate, the main building being a handsome long factory building of 1916, with a classical doorway in a central projecting bay; it was built for Heaths, navigational and scientific instrument makers founded at Erith 1845, who amalgamated with W F Stanley Co Ltd, tool and instrument makers, in 1926. (The future use of the building is uncertain, as the firm of Stanleys has recently closed.)

At the beginning of **Lannoy Road** alongside the site are short terraces of houses built for workers at Heaths c1917. The terraces further along the road were built earlier, c1891.

13. Daisy Munns House, a well-designed residential building of 1978, neatly rounding the corner of Avery Hill Road and Merchland Road.

14. Merchland Road has on both sides a number of substantial late 19th century houses, gabled and with ground floor bay windows.

15. Sparrows Lane. At the end of this road, built 1929 on the route of an old lane to Sparrows Farm, a footpath of the Green Chain Walk leads directly ahead to Avery Hill Park *(see Eltham 52E)*. To the left at this point is the training ground of Charlton Athletic Football Club, and to the right the Sparrows Farm Leisure Centre and sports grounds of the University of Greenwich, on the site of Sparrows Farm.

16. *Theobalds Cottages, 62/74 Avery Hill Road, a terrace of old cottages, the only survivors of the hamlet of Pope Street. Despite the date 1817 on the front, they basically date back at least to the 1760s. The porches are modern additions. No 74A was an addition in similar style of c1996.

NEW ELTHAM

Suggested Walk

It is recommended that the suggested walk be followed in conjunction with the Gazetteer and the maps, and that the Gazetteer be consulted at each location. All locations described in the Gazetteer are covered.
The walk begins and ends at New Eltham Station. Try to make advance arrangements - see the gazetteer -to see the interior of All Saints Church. Distance approx three kilometres.

On leaving **New Eltham Station (1)** turn left along Footscray Road, and left again into **Blanmerle Road** to see **nos 2/4 (2)**. Retrace steps to Footscray Road, and turn left. Continue, passing **The Beehive (3)** to the right and **Wyborne School (4)** to the left, until you reach a small triangular green with a finger signpost on the left. The housing development to your left is **Clare Corner (5)**.

Turn left along Green Lane to the terrace formed by nos 84/136, **Victoria Cottages (6)**. Cross the road to **Cambridge Green**, which is part of the Clare Corner development. Continue to the junction with Footscray Road, turn right and return to the crossroads and New Eltham Station.

Pass the Station and **New Eltham Library (7)**, then turn right along **Southwood Road (8)**, continuing as far as **nos 86/104 (8A)**. Return along Southwood Road and take the last road on the right before the crossroads, Bercta Road, leading to **All Saints Church (9)**; try to see the interior.

Continue round Bercta Road and turn right along Footscray Road, passing **nos 468/472 (10)**, formerly **The Grange**, and continue as far as the **milestone (11)**, then return to the crossroads. Turn right along Avery Hill Road. Passing **Stanleys (12)** on the left, continue to **Daisy Munns House (12)** on the right. Go down **Merchland Road (14)** a short way, then return to Avery Hill Road and turn right. Continue to nos 62/74, **Theobalds Cottages (16)**, then cross the road and bear left. Pass **Sparrows Lane (15)**; if you have time, go to the end, then retrace steps. Continue to the crossroads and New Eltham Station.

MOTTINGHAM

Introduction

Historically Mottingham developed as an extension of Eltham, but it has taken on a separate identity since the opening of the railway station in 1866, and even more so since the opening in 1923 of Sidcup Road which separates it from Eltham.

Mottingham now forms an irregular oblong, over two kilometres long, to the south of Sidcup Road. At the western end is the old hamlet, still surrounded by fields and open space. In the centre is the core of late Victorian development, which followed the arrival of the railway, now surrounded by interwar housing. At the eastern end the area opens out to embrace the vast Mottingham and Coldharbour Estates.

Early history

There is no evidence of a Roman settlement, though the foundations of a Roman building, probably a bath house, were discovered in Mottingham in 1939. There is however documentary evidence of a Saxon settlement at Mottingham, as it is mentioned in a charter of 862 AD.

During the reign of Edward I Mottingham passed from the manor of Lewisham to the manor of Eltham, which became a royal manor. But, as an extra-parochial hamlet, Mottingham did not become part of the parish of Eltham.

The hamlet was on the lane from Lee to Chislehurst. Its early development was around Mottingham Lane, on higher ground above the River Quaggy. (What is now called Mottingham Village is a post-railway development.)

In the 18th century there were two large houses on the south side of Mottingham Lane - Mottingham House and Fairy Hall. Mottingham House was a late 18th century rebuild of a Tudor building called Mottingham Place; it was demolished in 1969. Fairy Hall dates back to at least 1720; it was rebuilt in 1865, and has survived as the main building of Eltham College. At the eastern end of Mottingham Lane, the first Porcupine Inn was established in 1688.

All around was farmland. Mottingham Farm was on the north side of Mottingham Lane. To the south was Court Farm (of which Fairy Hall Cottage is a surviving farm building), to the east Chapel Farm and Coldharbour Farm. To the north and west were the farms of Middle Park and Horn Park, in the old parklands of Eltham Palace.

The coming of the railway

More large villas, including The Grange and The Chantry, which both survive, had been built in Mottingham Lane even before the railway arrived in 1866. The opening of Eltham Station (it was not renamed Mottingham Station until 1927) was followed by the construction of a road, to be called Court Road, from Eltham through Chapel Farm to Mottingham Road, and the present Mottingham Village began to take shape.

The short streets to the west of Mottingham Road were developed from 1870. The parish church arrived in 1880, on a site previously part of Chapel Farm and isolated from other developments at the time.

A particularly attractive housing development called West Chislehurst Park followed. It started at the eastern end of the street now called Grove Park Road in 1879, and continued into the street now called West Park in the late 1880s. The first parade of shops in Mottingham Road dates from 1894.

Modern growth

But the area did not experience intensive development until the 1930s. With the opening of further shopping parades in 1935, Mottingham Village became a minor shopping centre. The Mottingham part of Court Road, which previously consisted of only a few houses in addition to the church, became fully built up, together with the streets to its east. On the west side of Mottingham Road the London County Council built the large Mottingham Estate.

In the postwar period there was more development to the east. The vast Coldharbour Estate was built from 1947 by the Metropolitan Borough of Woolwich, and in 1973 the Greater London Council acquired Geffery's Court, the former Ironmongers Almshouse, to become the centrepiece of a smaller estate.

MOTTINGHAM

Gazetteer

(See map on page 62)

1. Mottingham Station. Opened in 1866 when the Dartford Loop Line was laid down, it was originally named Eltham Station. Its location so far south of Eltham was because the tenant of Eltham Lodge at the time, Anne Wood *(see Eltham 16)*, would not agree to the railway crossing Great Park. It was renamed Eltham & Mottingham in 1892, and Mottingham in 1927.

The weatherboarded building on the north (down) side is basically part of the original station of 1866. The present main station building on the south (up) side is of 1957, though a fragment of the original weatherboarded building of 1866 survives to the left. The footbridge is late 19th century.

2. St Andrews Church, Court Road. A rather uninspired Victorian Gothic church in red brick designed by Edward Clarke 1880. The present chancel was added in 1912, and the porch in 1913.

However, the **interior** *(contact the Rectory next door at 233 Court Road, or phone 020-8857 1691)*, with its wagon roof, great chancel arch and acutely pointed transept arches, is quite striking. Note the reredos with its painting, which is a copy of an altarpiece by Perugino, the original of which is in the National Gallery.

The east window was bricked up after wartime destruction. The two stained glass windows in the north transept are of interest: the central panel of the window to the left is made up of fragments salvaged from the destroyed east window, and the window to the right has a panel of a modern scene with a red London bus.

The rather rustic **Rectory** with a Gothic doorway next door dates from 1886.

3. *West Park. A wide and exceedingly handsome road, lined by horse chestnut trees. Apart from Priory Leas, a block of flats of 1973 at the eastern end, the entire north side consists of large, distinctive and highly attractive houses built 1887-89. Most are detached houses, there are only two pairs. All the houses have prominent gables, either tile-hung or patterned brick, and many have a fine sequence of windows. Other good decorative features on many of the houses include rustic timber porches, intriguing (sometimes somewhat grotesque) pargetting, and intricate brickwork. Inset into the boundary wall outside no 31 is a late Victorian letter-box.

On the south side nos 2/10 and 14/24, mostly pairs, are a similar group, also built 1887-89. At the eastern end no 56, a solitary survivor from another such group, is flanked by postwar flats and houses. Many of these original houses have doorways recessed within a Tudor porch. Nos 12 and 26/32, which have many similar features, were added after 1895. Other houses are modern. The office and restaurant at the western end, probably of the early 1890s, are stylistically different, with their half-timbered gables and oriel windows, but form an interesting and harmonious prelude to the houses in West Park.

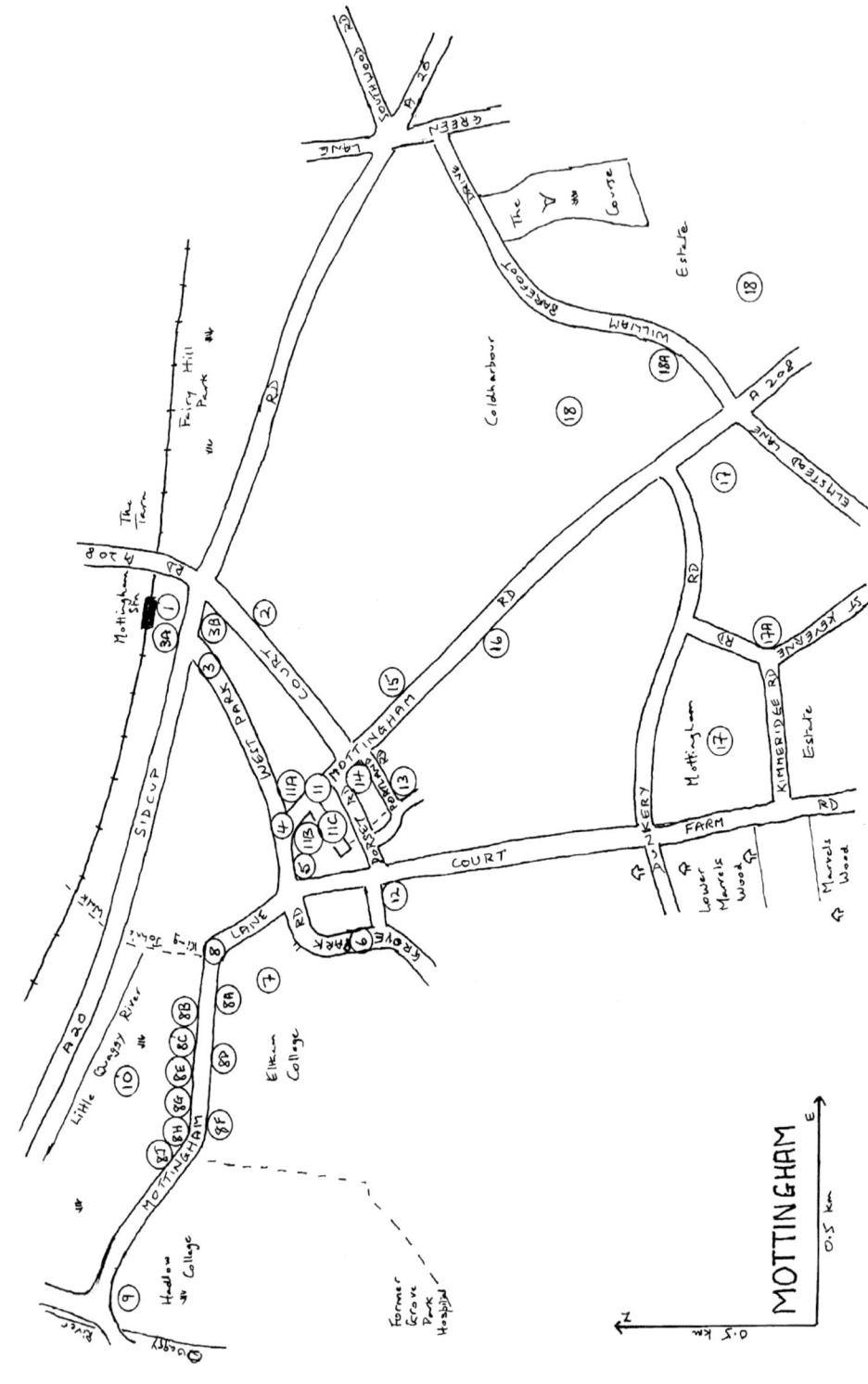

Near the east end of West Park, the large gabled houses at **501/503 Sidcup Road** (3A) and **202/208 Court Road** (3B) were part of the same development.

West Park originally formed part of a street called West Chislehurst Park, which extended west to include the western part of the present Mottingham Road *(see 5)* and the eastern part of the present Grove Park Road *(see 6)*.

4. The war memorial, a hexagon of Doric columns designed by George Hubbard 1922, serves as a roundabout and is a focal point for the area.

5. 2 Mottingham Road is a fine white Arts & Crafts house with brown weatherboarded gables and fine horizontal windows, of 1911. Nos 4/6 are a pair in similar style.

6. Grove Park Road has at its eastern end some attractive late 19th century houses. It formed part of West Chislehurst Park, but development here started in 1879, earlier than the houses now in West Park *(see 3)*.

On the south side, no 1, of 1880, is a handsome house, with a polygonal brick tower, and pargetting in the gable and over the windows. No 3, of 1879, has a fine projecting central section, a half-timbered gable and a Tudor porch. No 5 is modern. Tower House, no 7, of 1880, is an impressive house, with a polygonal brick tower and a doorway recessed in a Tudor porch.

Round a bend in the road, nos 25/33 are five large gabled Arts & Crafts houses, probably c1890, with some attractive sequences of windows. Opposite, no 8, of 1907, has nice horizontal windows; nos 10/12, probably c1907, have rustic wooden porches and upper floors linked by a wooden balcony; nos 14/16, probably c1903, have horizontal windows in the gable and gabled dormers.

7. Eltham College, Grove Park Road, is a complex of buildings with very extensive grounds. At the centre is a classical building of 1856, which was a rebuild of an 18th century building known as Fairy Hall.

> From 1889 to 1910 Fairy Hall was occupied by the Royal Naval School (which had moved from the building of the present Goldsmiths College at New Cross). In 1911 the School for the Sons of Missionaries (which had occupied the present Church Army headquarters in Blackheath Village) moved there, retaining the name Eltham College, which had in fact been used by the Naval School in its latter years.

The main building has a classical portico and parapet, with a prominent tower behind. At the bottom of the front facade is the foundation stone of the Royal Naval School; the stone is of 1843 and was moved here in 1889. To the right is a large plane tree, one of the largest in the London area. Further to the right is the Chapel of 1903, with patterned brickwork and great semi-circular arched windows.

The **interior** of the main building has a splendid central hall, with a classical gallery, and a glazed and intricately decorated roof. Behind the main building is a partly arcaded quadrangle.

The building is not normally open to the public, but there is a good view of the main front from Grove Park Road. It may be worth telephoning 020-8857 1455 to see whether it is possible to make an arrangement to see the interior.

8. *Mottingham Lane. A winding road, which was the original village street of Mottingham and still retains a rural atmosphere. The old path between Mottingham and Eltham, King John's Walk *(see Eltham 5)*, joins Mottingham Lane near its eastern end. The road contains a surprising variety of house design. Note, from east to west:

64 - MOTTINGHAM

Colview Court (8A), a modern development of 1969; it is on the site of Mottingham Place, a building of 1560, which was replaced in the late 18th century by Mottingham House, demolished 1969. An outbuilding to Mottingham House, probably c1855, survives as part of **Old Chapel**, a white building to the west which in 1903 was converted to a chapel. Other houses further west - **Culver** and **St Vincent** - were also buildings, probably c1855, in the grounds, but substantially altered (with some striking brickwork) during the period between 1890s and 1926, when Mottingham House was used as a Roman Catholic school and orphanage.

The Copse (8B), a red brick Arts & Crafts house, probably c1890, extended to the east to make it L-shaped, with an entrance in the angle, in 1911. Inset into the gatepost outside is a late Victorian **wall letter-box**.

Cedar Mount (8C), a development of 1959, which retains at the eastern end a Gothic style coach-house from a house on the site called Cedar Mount, probably c1880.

The Chantry (8D), a rather strange and gloomy house, probably c1860, multi-gabled, with Tudor and Gothic windows, and fanciful chimneypots. Contemporary coach-house to the east.

Mottingham Farm Riding Centre (8E). This was a working farm until the 1950s, but it is now used as riding stables and incorporates an extensive network of fields extending north to Sidcup Road *(see 10)*. The white building to the right of the entrance is the first farmhouse of 1850, and some farm buildings c1900 have survived. **Cley Cottage**, a short distance to the west, was built as a new farmhouse; it retains a Crown plaque showing the construction date of 1862.

The Grange (8F). A large and dignified classical house c1860, with a graceful entrance stairway and intricately decorated door-hood to the west, and fine ornamental railings to the main floor windows; much extended, it is now Eltham College Junior School. To the east, projecting forward, is a contemporary outbuilding with round-headed arches, formerly known as Grange Cottage, extended later to the east. Further west, behind the original iron gates, is **Grange Lodge**, also c1860, with bargeboarded gables on the front and the sides. The entrance drive which once led from the Lodge to the west entrance of the Grange has been developed with modern houses.

Alongside Grange Lodge a pleasant rural footpath, part of the Green Chain Walk, passes between the Eltham College grounds and riding stable grounds, and emerges in Marvels Lane, Grove Park, alongside the River Quaggy and adjacent to the housing estate on the site of the former Grove Park Hospital.

Norlesden House (8G), an extraordinary fantasy house, probably c1875, with Gothic window and doorway arches in polychrome brick, a Gothic oriel and narrow Gothic windows. A contemporary coach-house adjoins.

Fairmount (8H). This house of 1876 has a London County Council blue plaque to the cricketer W. G. Grace, who lived here from 1909 till his death in 1915. Note the gable with its strange bargeboard made up of circular discs.

The Lodge and **Woodcroft** (now also called Hilltop House) **(8J)** are basically the lodge and an outbuilding, much altered, of a house called Woodcroft (probably of the 1860s, now demolished), which was on the site of the present Carters Hill Close (a development of 1961).

9. **Hadlow College Mottingham Centre**, incorporating a garden centre.
The site was once part of the grounds of Mottingham Hall, a large house of the late 19th century. In 1899 the site became part of the grounds of Greenwich Workhouse, later Grove Park Hospital, though Mottingham Hall was not demolished until c1960.
In 1987 MacIntyre, an organisation arranging educational training for mentally handicapped persons, opened a nature reserve and garden centre here. In 1996 the site was taken over by Hadlow College, an associate college of the University of Greenwich, specialising in agricultural and horticultural studies.
Remaining from the old nature reserve is a circular rural walk of nearly a kilometre, which is pleasant but isolated and in places very overgrown. Starting to the right of the car park, it follows the banks of the Quaggy River, then continues through woodland and rough grassland, before returning to the entrance. The garden centre.is in the middle of the circle. Hadlow College plans to restore the nature reserve.

10. **The old Mottingham Farm fields.** A large network of fields stretching down to Sidcup Road, now used by riding stables; it was previously farmland of the old Mottingham Farm in Mottingham Lane *(see 8E)*.
The fields are watered by the Quaggy River, running alongside Mottingham Lane, and by its tributary, the Little Quaggy, running near Sidcup Road. They join together in a field at the western end. The riverside environment of the Little Quaggy is particularly pleasant and natural. The Quaggy continues on the other side of Sidcup Road into Harmony Wood *(see Eltham 13)*.

11. **Mottingham Village.** A small shopping centre in Mottingham Road. It was not the original village of Mottingham, but has a sort of village atmosphere. This is perhaps because of the houses (a few of which have modern shopfronts) on the south side which were built after the coming of the railway in 1866 and the subsequent extension of Court Road.
The earliest shops are at **37/45 Mottingham Road (11A)**, dating from 1894, but it did not really become a shopping street until after 1935, when another shopping parade was built. By the small library of 1968 is an abstract concrete sculpture by Carol Morgan.
The **Porcupine Inn (11B)**, 24 Mottingham Road, at the west end, is a building of 1922, looking like a great suburban house. This is at least the third inn on the site; the earliest was of 1688.
Devonshire Road (11C), a short cul-de-sac, has many terraced cottages c1870, and at no 33 a fine detached house with gabled porch and dormers closing the view from Mottingham Road. At the end a footpath leads southwards across Dorset Road to **Portland Road**, where there are similar terraced cottages c1870.

12. **Fairy Hall Cottage**, 12 Court Farm Road. Originally a farm building, part of Court Farm, which belonged to Fairy Hall. It is the oldest building in Mottingham, and may be at least as old as 1750. The cottage is basically one-storey, and has a nice doorway with a pediment which springs out of the roof; it has lost its thatched roof.

13. **Haworth Graves**, Beaconsfield Road. Two late Victorian gravestones, with a slab reading 'The family mausoleum of Thomas Chester Haworth of Eltham'. He was Surveyor to Eltham Parish Council, and pioneered the construction of a modern drainage system in Eltham; he died in 1887. The mausoleum itself, built in 1875, in

which seven members of the family were buried, was destroyed during the last war; it was an unusual phenomenon on such a small isolated site.

14. Mottingham Methodist Church, a small stone church of 1883 with three tall Gothic windows facing east, and a nice pyramidal bellcote on top.

15. Church of Our Lady Help of Christians, a Roman Catholic stone church of 1933, notable for its numerous Gothic lancet windows.

16. *Geffery's Court, 158 Mottingham Road. A very imposing building in a renaissance style by George Hubbard 1912, of red brick with ample stone dressings, almost baroque with wonderful classical detailing. Note the fine and intricate iron gates fronting the road.

> It was built as Geffryes Homes, the almshouse of the Company of Ironmongers, which was moved here from the building in Shoreditch which has since 1914 been the Geffrye Museum. It became part of a Greater London Council housing estate in 1974.

It is quite an elaborate composition, worthy of close study. The projecting central block is surmounted by a large pediment; the handsome doorcase has fluted columns and other fine ornamentation, with an upper stage ornamented with cherubs heads and other lavish detail. On both sides of this central block are sections which recede until you come to two long wings, each with handsome porches and fine doorcases. There is a dentilled cornice all the way round, both front and rear.

The rear, accessible through the central doorway, also has a fine doorcase surmounted by a large pediment; in each flanking wing are wide elaborate porches and a handsome doorcase. The sections which project at the front are matched by sections which recede at the rear. At each end of the flanking wings, further classical wings project at right angles, and there is an attractive garden in between.

17. Mottingham Estate. A large and spaciously laid out 'cottage' estate developed on part of the site of Court Farm by the London County Council from 1935 to 1939. The estate incorporates several attractive greens and two small belts of woodland, Marvels Wood and Lower Marvels Wood. Some fine old oaks survive in Dunkery Road near the junction with Mottingham Road.

The red brick **Church of St Edward the Confessor (17A)**, St Keverne Road, is a focal point on the estate, its tall square tower facing down the shopping street of Kimmeridge Road. It was built in 1958, though the church hall and vicarage on either side are both of the 1930s. Prominent on the tower is an effigy of St Edward. The **interior** *(contact the vicarage next door)* is distinctive, with imposing arches.

18. Coldharbour Estate. A large and spacious estate developed on the site of Coldharbour Farm by the Metropolitan Borough of Woolwich from 1947. It is sliced in two by a major road, William Barefoot Drive, where the small shopping centre and community buildings are located.

The estate was planned as a 'garden suburb', and there are many attractive greens. From the open space at **The Course** there is a magnificent view towards Eltham and Shooters Hill, including a particularly impressive distant view of Eltham Lodge.

St Albans Church (18A), a small red brick church designed by Ralph Covell 1953, has a nice square tower and gently bowed east window, and is linked by an arcade to the original vicarage. The **interior** *(phone the Vicar on 020-8851 4824)* is worth viewing for the splendid stained glass in the east window by Carter Shapland.

MOTTINGHAM

Suggested Walk

It is recommended that the suggested walk be followed in conjunction with the Gazetteer and the map, and that the Gazetteer be consulted at each location for a detailed description. Most locations described in the Gazetteer are covered; the Mottingham and Coldharbour Estates have not been included, as they would add too much to the length of the walk.
  The walk begins and ends at Mottingham Station; it follows a more or less circular route, so can be joined at any location. Distance approx 5 kilometres Try to make advance arrangements - see the Gazetteer - to see the interior of St Andrews Church.

On leaving **Mottingham Station (1)**, turn right along Court Road and cross Sidcup Road at the traffic lights, then turn right. Turn left into **West Park (3)** and walk to the end, noting the **war memorial (4)**. Continue, passing **2 Mottingham Road (5)**, and bear right into **Mottingham Lane (8)**.

Keeping to the north side, note on the opposite side **Colview Court (8A)** and other buildings on the site of Mottingham House, then **The Chantry (8D)**, **The Grange (8F)** and **Grange Lodge**. Continue downhill along Mottingham Lane until you reach **Hadlow College Mottingham Centre (9)**. The **Mottingham Farm fields (10)** are opposite.

Retrace steps up Mottingham Lane, keeping to the south side. Note on the opposite side **The Lodge** and **Woodcroft (8J)**, **Fairmount (8H)**, **Norlesden House (8G)**, the old buildings of **Mottingham Farm (8E)**, **Cedar Mount (8C)** and **The Copse (8B)**, then continue to the crossroads. Turn right along **Grove Park Road (6)** to see nos 1 & 7 and other houses, and for the view of **Eltham College (7)**.

Return to the crossroads and bear right into **Mottingham Village (11),** noting the **Porcupine Inn (11B)** on the right. Turn right into **Devonshire Road (11C)** and take the footpath at the end on the left, then turn right into Dorset Road. Note **Fairy Hall Cottage (12)** opposite at the end, and return, bearing right down Portland Crescent. At the beginning of Beaconsfield Road to the right are the **Haworth Graves (13)**. Continue down Portland Road to Mottingham Road, note **Mottingham Methodist Church (14)** on the corner, then turn right.

Continue, passing the **Church of Our Lady Help of Christians (15)**, until you reach **Geffery's Court (16)** on the right; go through the central doorway to see the rear. Retrace steps along Mottingham Road past Portland Road, and turn right along Court Road. Halfway down on the right is **St Andrews Church (2)**; try to see the interior. Continue, noting **nos 202/208 (3B)** on the left at the end, to the traffic lights. Cross over Sidcup Road and you are quickly back at Mottingham Station.

KIDBROOKE

Introduction

Kidbrooke is nowadays generally considered to be the area bounded to the west by Kidbrooke Park Road, to the north by Shooters Hill Road, to the east by Greenwich Cemetery, and stretching south along Rochester Way on the way to Eltham. In the south-west corner there is a bulge across the Rochester Way Relief Road and the Bexleyheath Line to embrace the Ferrier Estate and Sutcliffe Park. It is a vast area, without any clear focal point or cohesion.

But the old parish of Kidbrooke was even larger. It stretched from Kidbrooke Park Road westwards to St Germans Place on the edge of Blackheath, an area which is covered by the gazetteer which follows. The south side of Shooters Hill Road, mostly part of the old parish, is included in the gazetteer, and a number of houses and a church on the north side of the road, which were outside the old parish, are also included. The old parish also extended to cover the southern part of the Cator Estate in Blackheath, but this area is not included in the gazetteer; nor are Morden College and the Heath itself, which were just outside the old parish boundary.

The Kid Brook streams

Three streams, tributaries of the Quaggy River - the Upper, Mid and Lower Kid Brook - flow through the area, though almost entirely now in underground conduits. All three rise at different points near Shooters Hill Road, though the source in each case is hidden.

Only the Mid Kid Brook can readily be seen in the area, in Kidbrooke Park Road opposite St John Fisher Church; it can also be seen at two points on the Cator Estate in Blackheath - entering and leaving the pond on the Brooklands Estate, and at 24 Parkgate. A short section of the Lower Kid Brook can be seen before it joins the River Quaggy on the northern edge of the Roan School playing fields on Kidbrooke Park Road. The Upper Kid Brook is not visible at any point, though the shallow dip where Westbrook Road joins Kidbrooke Grove and Kidbrooke Park Road betrays its underground course.

Old Kidbrooke

The village of Kidbrooke, with its own church and village green, was in existence at least by the early 12th century. But from the early 15th century it went into a decline, probably caused by the Black Death. The church became derelict, and there was no parish church again until St James was built in 1867 on a different site.

A large part of Kidbrooke Green has survived, otherwise there are no traces of the former village. The route of the old village lane, where the medieval church and farm buildings once stood and which led to Eltham, has survived in Brook Lane, and also in Kidbrooke Lane in Eltham; between these points it followed roughly the route of

Rochester Way. An old footpath runs through the northern grounds of Morden College, then crosses Kidbrooke Grove and ends in Kidbrooke Park Road near the junction with Brook Lane; this may originally have been a continuation of Long Pond Road, now once more a footpath rather than a road across Blackheath.

19th century Kidbrooke

Before 1800 the only major building in the area, though just outside the old parish of Kidbrooke, was Morden College, an almshouse attributed to Sir Christopher Wren, built overlooking Blackheath in 1695.

Domestic development began with the construction c1812 of Kidbrooke Lodge, just to the north of the College and at the southern end of the present St Germans Place; the house was demolished in 1902, and Kidbrooke Gardens and Liskeard Gardens were laid out in the grounds. The remainder of St Germans Place was developed from 1823, and the western part of Shooters Hill Road from 1825. The houses built in this part of the area were of a very high standard.

The extension eastwards of Shooters Hill Road continued up to the 1860s, when the northern part of Kidbrooke Park Road, Hervey Road and Eastbrook Road were developed. Kidbrooke Grove was developed from 1871.

At the eastern end of the area Greenwich Cemetery was laid out in 1856. The former Royal Herbert Hospital was built for the Royal Artillery on the site of Kidbrooke Common in 1865, and the former Brook Hospital alongside in 1896. The two hospitals have been in recent years converted to housing estates, though in the case of the Brook the development is not yet complete.

By the turn of the century development was still largely confined to the northern and north-west fringes of the area. Even after Kidbrooke Station was opened in 1895 on the Bexleyheath Line, further housing was slow to follow, and the central area of Kidbrooke continued as farmland.

Suburban development

The rural landscape, with many fields still being farmed, remained right through the interwar period; from this period, Oakhaven Villas, a pair of farmworkers houses of the 1930s belonging to Manor Farm, still survive in altered form by the Kidbrooke School playing fields near the western end of Dursley Road. However, in the early 1930s the construction of the Shooters Hill By-pass, or Rochester Way, did lead to a surge in housing development - further eastwards along Shooters Hill Road and further southwards along Kidbrooke Park Road, and in and around the long new roads of Wricklemarsh Road and Broad Walk.

The spread of housing continued soon after the end of the war, when the London County Council built in the late 1940s extensive cottage-style estates, pleasant if rather monotonous - the Evelyn, Brook and Lower Brook Estates - which more or less completely covered the remaining fields of Kidbrooke (apart from those which became sports grounds).

The more thrusting Ferrier Estate was built to the south of the railway by the Greater London Council in 1974, largely on the site of a former RAF depot. In 1988 the Rochester Way Relief Road was completed, running alongside the railway.

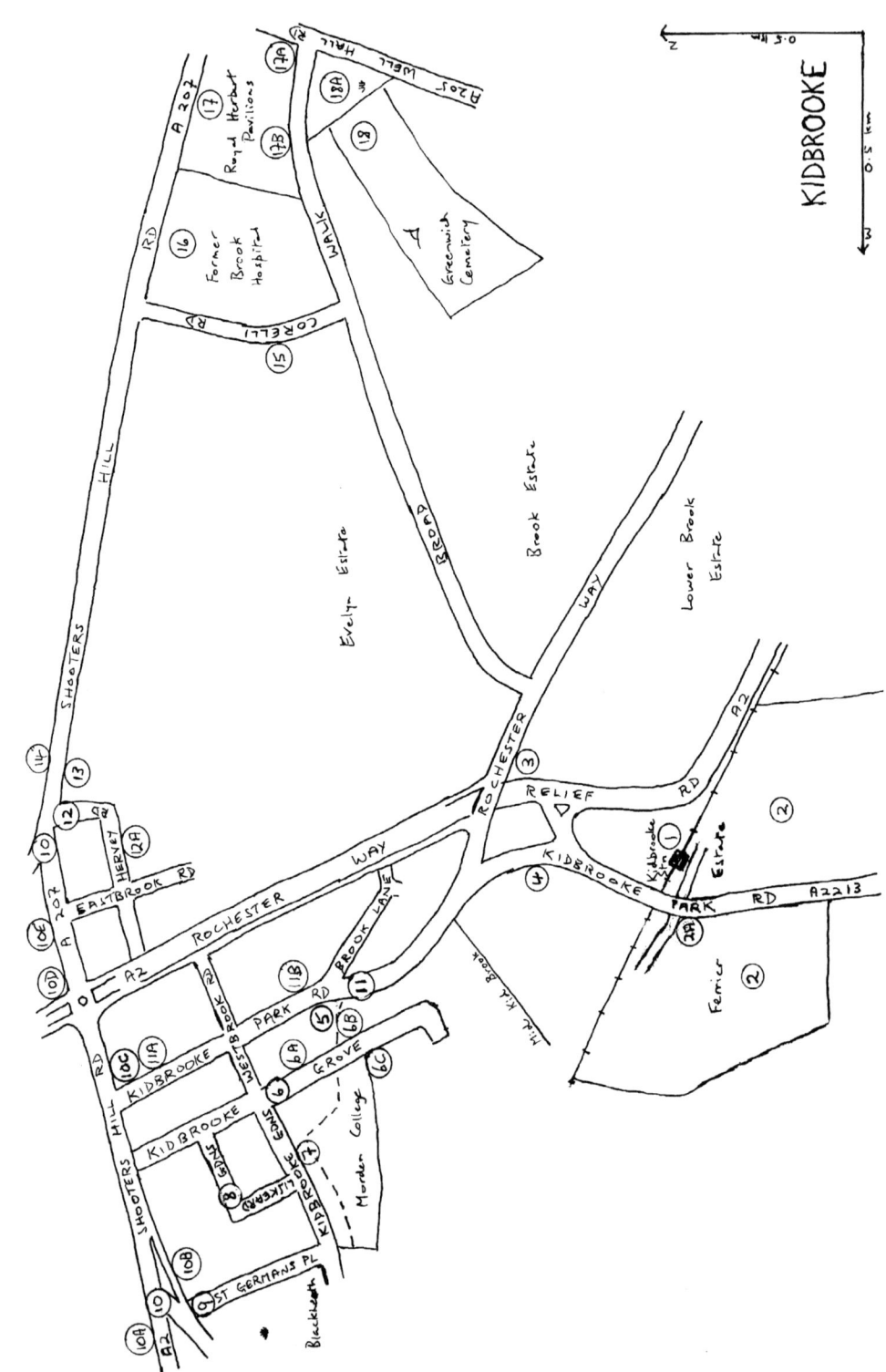

KIDBROOKE

Gazetteer

1. Kidbrooke Station. The station was originally opened in 1895 on the Bexleyheath Line; the present buildings are of 1994 and basic. From the nearby road bridge over the railway there is a view to the west of the **railway tunnel** under Blackheath Park.

2. Ferrier Estate. A massive concrete estate straddling Kidbrooke Park Road built by the Greater London Council, completed 1974. It occupies a large part of the site of RAF Depot Kidbrooke, which opened 1917 and closed 1965; the station was noted for radio masts during the interwar period and for barrage balloons during the second world war. The depot had its own private railway linking many parts of the site, with a siding from the main Bexleyheath Line just west of the present bridge over the railway; no traces now remain. From the twin-arched road bridge (**2A**) at Kidbrooke Park Road, you can look down on the main road through the estate which at this point was laid down in the track-bed of the RAF private railway.

The concrete tower blocks of the estate look quite dramatic from afar, but on the estate itself the environment can be overpowering. However, a process of renewal and replanning, with attractive landscaping of the ten squares on the estate, was carried out in the early 1990s. Further changes and improvements to the environment of the estate are likely in the next few years, and these may well be on a major scale.

3. Kidbrooke Green. The old village green was originally more extensive. The remaining section, an area of grassed open space, now occupies the angle between the old Rochester Way and the new Rochester Way Relief Road. To the west is a nature reserve with a large pond, but public access is restricted.

4. Thomas Tallis School, Kidbrooke Park Road. A basic modernist school of 1971. On the east front, facing the road, is **Time and Space**, an extraordinary multi-part sculpture by Margaret Higginson 1991, comprising the sun, the moon, a comet, the zodiac signs, a Ptolemaic revolving instrument, and (on a chimney) three sundials.

5. St James Church, Kidbrooke Park Road. A Victorian Gothic ragstone church designed by Newman & Billing 1867. It was restored after substantial war damage by Thomas Ford in 1955, with a new green copper roof and spire (though not nearly so tall as the original stone spire).

The **interior** *(contact the vicarage at the rear of the church, or phone 020-8856 3438)* is pleasant and spacious, with sharply pointed arches. Note the postwar stained glass, exotically multi-coloured, by Edwards & Powell in the large east window.

6. *Kidbrooke Grove. A very wide and highly attractive road, lined by tall lime trees; it is notable for a number of fine Edwardian houses, though the earliest houses date from 1871. It forms a cul-de-sac at both ends, with road access only in the middle; at the southern end it turns a corner to come sharply up against a brick wall, beyond which is the eastern end of Blackheath Park.

Of the northern half, the east side retains a late Victorian character with rows of tall houses. The houses on the west side are late Victorian as far as Liskeard Gardens, and Edwardian beyond.

The southern half is perhaps more interesting. By 1914 there were only seven houses - the east side was taken up with two late Victorian mansions (originally called Morden Grange and Stonefield) in large grounds, separated by an old footpath; the west side had five Edwardian villas (two designed by leading architects). More intensive development on both sides came mostly in the 1930s, and also after 1945.

Note in particular, from north to south:

Nos 3/7, built in 1871. No 3 is impressive, with an amazing variety of window shapes. Nos 5/7 have unusual carvings of fish on the rainwater head. (Nos 36/38 Shooters Hill Road were part of the same development - *see 10.*)

Nos 4/6, an interesting pair of 1871, with a remarkable frieze under the eaves, consisting of plasterwork incised with figures of animals and weird patterns. Nos 2 and 12 were originally the coach-houses for this pair.

Inset into the front wall of no 11 (a large and solid house of 1873) is a Victorian **wall letter-box**.

Nos 31/33 are a fine Edwardian pair of 1908-09. No 31 is neo-Georgian; and no 33, larger and imaginatively asymmetrical, was designed by Thomas Norman Dinwiddy, son of the more famous Thomas Dinwiddy.

No 37, an Edwardian neo-Georgian house of 1905 designed by Sir Reginald Blomfield, with a prominent shell hood over the front door.

No 39 (Morden House), an Edwardian red brick classical house of 1912 designed by John James Joass and John Belcher, large and handsome, with fine detailing.

Nos 36/42 (6A), reached by a short lane (opposite no 39). Here is an extraordinary phenomenon. Nos 36/38 are substantially the ground floor (though with extensions) of a mansion of 1888, built as **Morden Grange** to a design by John Belcher, and at that time accessed by a driveway from Westbrook Road. In 1921 the upper floors were sliced off and became in part the basis of the fabric of **no 26**, at the junction with Westbrook Road. No 40 was converted from the stables. No 42 is postwar.

No 58 (6B), a substantial mansion of 1877, originally called **Stonefield**, with a turret and a conservatory, and lots of quirky classical detailing. It is now a family centre. From 1920 to 1954 it was a well-known and pioneering maternity clinic run by Dr William White and Dr Cyril Pink.

No 73 (6C), an attractive Arts & Crafts house of 1903, red brick, with bold white gabled upper floors over the canted bay windows at each end. This was the earliest of the Edwardian villas of Kidbrooke Grove.

7. 22 Kidbrooke Gardens. An imposing Edwardian mansion of 1905 in 'Queen Anne' style, designed by Arthur Torrance, with balconies at front and rear, fine bows, and other interesting decorative features.

From the road there is a good view of the frontage of Morden College, an almshouse of 1695 attributed to Sir Christopher Wren.

8. Liskeard Gardens. An attractive road, consisting mainly of houses in a variety of Edwardian styles built from 1906 to 1912.

Perhaps the most interesting house is on a bend in the road, no 19, c1907; it is in a warm mix of orange and red bricks, with the section containing the fine entrance porch recessed between two bold projecting sections. It was designed by Samuel Dottridge, who lived at no 21, a distinctive Arts & Crafts house, also c1907.

9. *St Germans Place. Viewed from afar this street, with Shooters Hill looming in the distance, presents quite a dramatic eastern edge to Blackheath. From here the views over Blackheath are spectacular. The buildings are mainly of the 1820s, with some postwar intrusions. The older houses are, from north to south:

Nos 1 & 2, small brick houses c1825, similar to the 'tea caddy houses' of Shooters Hill Road *(see 10B)*, though there has been a later extension to no 2.

Christs College, no 4, an attractive and well-designed brick building. It has been in use as a school almost continuously since it was built in 1823. The separate proprietory chapel of 1823 was demolished in 1967 (after substantial war damage); nos 5a/e of 1969 are now on the site.

No 9, a handsome house c1825 with a distinctive bow, attractive doorcase and iron balcony.

Nos 10/13, two stuccoed cubic pairs c1826.

No 14, a highly attractive stuccoed house c1829 with an elegant iron balcony.

Nos 15/16, a very large pair c1826 with fine porches, dominating the distant view. The top storey of each house are additions, probably early 20th century.

10. *Shooters Hill Road. This long road extends from Blackheath past the motorway roundabout right up to the junction with Academy Road, which leads to Woolwich, and Well Hall Road, which leads to Eltham. The western part has a concentration of impressive 19th century houses, built between 1825 and 1869.

The initial groups nos 1/35 form a very attractive and positive north-east edge to the Heath. Further east, the Heath narrows sharply to a triangular green, on which is an 18th century **milestone**, with replicas of 19th century iron plates reading 'London 6 miles' and 'Dartford 9 miles'. South of the green at this point are nos 2/20 with their distinctive shapes, the earliest houses on the road.

Beyond the green as far as the roundabout, the large and solid houses facing each other present a powerful and stately appearance when viewed as extended groups. They were built from 1846 to 1861, apart from the smaller houses of 1906 on either side of Vicarage Avenue. They are mostly pairs, though there are a number of detached houses with strong porches. On the north side many houses are stuccoed. The large trees in this section enhance the appeal. (The wide pedestrian way formed by Vicarage Avenue is due to the shallow depth of the railway tunnel between Blackheath and Charlton at this point.)

In the section beyond the motorway roundabout and extending to Hervey Road, there is a contrast in appearance between the north and the south sides of the road.

The south side is a continuation of the development to the west of the roundabout. (The pattern also continues for short distances along Eastbrook Road and Hervey Road.) The houses were built in the 1860s, and are generally solid and powerful, with quite an impact when seen as groups; a few houses have masks on the brackets under the eaves.

The north side of this section is more individual. It was mainly developed in the 1840s as part of **Sun Field**, an area which also embraces the rebuilt Sun in the Sands.

Beyond Hervey Road, the houses are modern. At the eastern end are the site of the former Brook Hospital, now being converted for housing, and the former Royal Herbert Hospital, already a housing development.

Note in particular, from west to east:
No 1 (Heath House), an attractive house of 1852 with a large conservatory and a powerful porch, occupying a prominent position overlooking the Heath. **Nos 3/5** are smaller, also of 1852.

*Nos 7/33 (10A), an extensive group of semi-detached houses built 1840-44, originally known as **Blackheath Terrace**. These highly attractive stuccoed houses are in the striking individual style (of which there are several examples in the Blackheath area) considered as influenced by Michael Searles. The main feature is a large shared pediment which serves to unify the pairs and make them appear as detached villas. Other features are - pilasters framing each house; entrances in lower wings on either side; small round-headed windows under the pediment.

No 35 is a picturesque house of 1854 with odd gables and bargeboards, its quasi-Tudor style being in vivid contrast to the adjacent houses.

No 37 is a handsome house of 1847 on a prominent site looking diagonally back to the Heath - note the elegantly detailed porch and pilasters.

Nos 2/20 (10B), a fine group of detached brick villas built 1826-32, with some added porches and linking extensions. Because of their shape, they are sometimes called the 'tea caddy' houses; they were originally known as **St Germans Terrace**. The adjacent villas, nos 22/26, built 1851-53, are less distinctive.

No 36 and **38**, on either side of Kidbrooke Grove. Built in 1869, they were the precursors of the Kidbrooke Grove development. Like 3/7 Kidbrooke Grove *(see 6)*, they have some interesting features, including a variety of window shapes and (on no 38) unusual carvings on the rainwater heads.

No 63 is an impressive detached house of 1851, rendered in pale green, with a strong porch, and in a slightly more fanciful style than other houses here.

Nos 69/71, a particularly handsome stuccoed pair of 1848.

Nos 91/103 are a fine series of detached houses with strong porches built 1858-60.

Nos 56/76 (10C), a development of 1853, originally known as **Kidbrooke Terrace**. Mostly large pairs, nos 60/66 being distinguished by rather grand bow windows; though no 72 is a handsome detached house with a central porch. The stables for no 56 have been converted to become 1a Kidbrooke Park Road *(see 11)*.

Beyond the motorway roundabout, from west to east:

No 90, a fantasy house of 1862, painted stark blue, with windows in various styles and quite extraordinary decorative stonework.

Sun in the Sands (10D), 123 Shooters Hill Road. A pub of 1842, with a modern ground floor, on the site of an older pub.

Nos 129/131, a small and attractive pair of 1843. Adjoining are **nos 133/139**, stuccoed pairs of 1842.

*Nos 141/155 (10E), an elegant terrace of bow-fronted brick houses of 1846, originally known as **Waterfield Terrace**, with deep eaves and round-headed dormers in distinctively shaped roofs.

Nos 157/163, a terrace of village-style cottages of 1840, with a continuous wooden loggia.

No 134, an impressive villa of 1862 with a strong porch.

11. Kidbrooke Park Road. This road was developed from 1866, and the northern part, as far as St James Church, consists largely of substantial late 19th century houses. Note in particular the following, all on the east side:

No 1a, a village-like building of 1853, converted from the original stables of 56 Shooters Hill Road *(see 10C)*. **Rosse Mews**, which is adjacent, is a genuine mews, with some houses converted from old coach-houses of Shooters Hill Road.

Nos 1/9 (11A), an attractive group designed by John Whichcord 1868-70, with nice decorative features including verandahs with elegant ironwork, rows of small round-headed windows, and towers over most of the entrances.

Nos 63/67 (11B), a group of attractive detached houses c1872, all with elegant ironwork embracing porch and verandah.

12. Hervey Road. The easternmost part of this road was developed from 1868, as a continuation of the development on the south side of that part of Shooters Hill Road. Of the remainder, the north side is largely Edwardian, and the south side largely interwar. Note in particular:

Nos 75/81, a group of large stuccoed houses of 1879.

Nos 45/73, Edwardian villas c1910, which have impact as a long group.

No 80 (12A), a house probably c1914, with a striking porch of Tuscan columns supporting a polygonal projecting bay; it stands out in an otherwise unremarkable sequence of interwar houses.

13. Arnold House, Shooters Hill Road. A residential home of 1983 in a pleasant vernacular style. It incorporates the dispensary of the old Charlton and Blackheath Cottage Hospital; this small appealing mock-Tudor building, designed by Philip Robson 1904, with its quatrefoil panels and oriel window has been nicely integrated. The adjacent surgery is also in a sympathetic style.

14. Blackheath and Charlton Baptist Church, Shooters Hill Road. A Gothic church in deep red brick, designed by Samuel Dottridge 1905. It has a prominent stumpy tower, with four corner gargoyles at the top. The tracery in the windows, particularly the large south window, is intricate and complex.

The **interior** *(the church may be accessible Monday to Friday mornings, otherwise contact 020-8856 0833)* was transformed in 1977 when it was split horizontally at the level of the former galleries, just below the main windows; the ground floor now consists of a modern church room and the baptistery, with the church on the first floor. The church interior is dominated by the original four great semi-circular arches and four columns with elaborate capitals.

15. Kidbrooke School, Corelli Road. A very large brick building designed by Slater, Uren & Pike of 1954, which was in fact London's first purpose-built comprehensive school. The view from Corelli Road is dominated by the great green roof of the assembly hall with its sharply swept down corners.

16. Former Brook Hospital. A large hospital of 1894-96, built as an infectious diseases hospital alongside the older Royal Herbert Hospital. The hospital closed at the end of 1995, and a housing development has already commenced, to be called **Brook Village,** in the south and west of the site. Access is from Broad Walk as well as from Shooters Hill Road.

A housing development in the north and east of the site is likely to commence in the near future. The development will retain a number of imposing original buildings and structures, all designed by Thomas Aldwinckle, as follows:

The Dutch-gabled **porters lodge**, and behind, two gabled buildings with similar decorative features - the larger building to the left the **administration block**, and the smaller building to the right the former **doctors quarters**. The prominent **water tower** and front boundary wall, built of red brick with black brick patterns. A range of red brick retaining wall has been preserved in the Brook Village development.

The ragstone building by the Shooters Hill Road entrance, vividly contrasting with the red brick wall, was originally a **pumping station** of the Kent Waterworks Co of 1863, though this use ceased after a new pumping station in Well Hall Road opened in 1922. In the wall by the entrance is a late Victorian **wall letter-box**.

17. *Royal Herbert Pavilions, Shooters Hill Road. The old Royal Herbert Hospital was built on Kidbrooke Common by Sir Douglas Galton in 1865 as the general hospital of the Artillery Garrison at Woolwich. The hospital was superbly converted in the 1990s to become a flatted housing estate. It is a dramatic but rather heavy building complex with a classical frontage. Note the massive stone entrance piers with ornamental lamp-holders, linked by quadrant railings to the main building.

> The design of the Royal Herbert Hospital was in its day considered pioneering, with wards in separate pavilions leading off long corridors. Galton was a nephew of Florence Nightingale, and she probably had a great influence on the design on her return at the end of the Crimean War. It was closed in 1978, when the Queen Elizabeth Hospital on Woolwich Common was opened, originally as a military hospital.

The large block fronting the main road, with a great round central arch in the middle of the rusticated entrance block, is the old administration building. Behind and on either side are seven two-storey pavilions at right angles; all the pavilions are linked on the upper floor by a corridor 230 metres long. The lower floor corridor has been altered in the conversion. In the central pavilion, which has a clock on its bold north front, a grand staircase leads to a first floor flat, converted from a large chapel.

In the grounds are two buildings c1865, both now converted for housing - **The Lodge (17A)**, formerly known as Herbert House, on Well Hall Road, and **259 Broad Walk (17B)**, fomerly the mortuary, though this is not easily visible behind the original high brick wall of the hospital.

Part of the grounds, to the west, are currently being developed for housing as **Brook Mews**, a mock-Georgian development incorporating a crescent.

Opposite the complex are **Victoria House**, formerly the Medical Officers Mess, an attractive curved red brick building of 1909, with terracotta ornamentation; and **Adair House**, of 1928, formerly nurses quarters, in severe classical style.

18. *Greenwich Cemetery. This cemetery, originally laid out in 1856, occupies a spectacular hill-top site, with magnificent views towards Central London and over the suburbs to the west. There are two Gothic stone chapels.

Not far from the entrance and immediately to the left of the main pathway is the tombstone of Nicholas Ogareff 1877; in fact his remains were moved to Russia, where he was declared a national hero, in 1966. Further along, occupying a dominant position, is the Great War Heroes Corner, with a fine memorial cross and a Commonwealth burial ground. At the far west end is a separate section for Norwegians who have died in Britain.

Outside the entrance to the cemetery is **King George's Field (18A)**, a large and attractive green with a clump of oak trees in the centre. Formerly part of Eltham Common *(see Shooters Hill 6)*, it was.dedicated to George V after his death in 1936.

KIDBROOKE

Suggested Walk

It is recommended that the suggested walk be followed in conjunction with the Gazetteer and the maps, and that the Gazetteer be consulted at each location for a detailed description. The walk concentrates on locations in the western part of the area; to include other locations would add too much to the length of the walk, but they can of course be visited separately.

The walk begins and ends at Kidbrooke Station. It follows a more or less circular route, so can be joined at any location. Distance approx four kilometres. NB. It is worth trying to make advance arrangements - see the Gazetteer - to see the interior of St James Church.

On leaving **Kidbrooke Station (1)**, note the **Ferrier Estate (2)** to the left, then turn right and proceed along Kidbrooke Park Road, bearing left at the traffic lights. Pass **Thomas Tallis School (4)** to the left, and continue along Kidbrooke Park Road for half a kilometre until you reach **St James Church (5)** on the left; try to see the interior.

Follow the footpath to the left just before the church through to **Kidbrooke Grove (6)**; **no 58 (6B)** is on the left and **no 73 (6C)** almost opposite. Turn right, passing **nos 37 & 39** on the left, and beyond the junction, **nos 31/33**. Turn left along **Liskeard Gardens (8)**, and on reaching Kidbrooke Gardens, note **no 22 (7)** opposite. Turn right and continue until you reach Blackheath. (Although Morden College is not described in the Gazetteer, it is worth noting that by turning left at this point and turning left again along a footpath, you will have a fine view of Morden College, an almshouse of 1695 attributed to Sir Christopher Wren.)

On reaching Blackheath, turn right and follow **St Germans Place (9)**. From **Christs College** there is a wide view over the Heath. At the end of St Germans Place, note **7/33 Shooters Hill Road (10A)** ahead and turn right along **Shooters Hill Road (10)**, noting the houses on both sides.

On reaching Kidbrooke Grove on the right, turn down to see **nos 3/7** on the right and **nos 4/6** on the left, then return and continue along Shooters Hill Road. Turn right down **Kidbrooke Park Road (11)**, noting **no 1a** and **nos 1/9 (11A)** to the left, and further down on the left, **nos 63/67 (11B)**. Then continue down Kidbrooke Park Road, past St James Church, until you are back at Kidbrooke Station.

SHOOTERS HILL

Introduction

The Romans built Watling Street, the road between London and Dover, across the top of Shooters Hill, and the main road today, the A207 to Dartford, still broadly follows its course. The slope is steep on the west side coming from Blackheath, but more gradual on the east side going towards Welling. The road was improved and widened by the New Cross Turnpike Trust between 1718 and 1817.

The summit of the hill at 132 metres (in Eaglesfield Park) is one of the highest points in Greater London, and its landmark, the water tower, is prominent from afar - on a clear day it can be seen from Tower Bridge, from Hampstead Heath, and from the North Downs. Nearer, from the centre of Blackheath, the hump of the hill looks impressive and dramatic.

Early history

There was a beacon on the hill (its site now in the grounds of the Memorial Hospital) from at least the 16th century onwards. For many centuries the area with its extensive and dense woods was known as the haunt of highwaymen.

At the end of the 18th century the buildings on Shooters Hill consisted of two taverns (predecessors of the present Bull and Red Lion), a few houses and Severndroog Castle, an extraordinary folly. (An even older tavern, the Catherine Wheel, was demolished c1778.) The largest house, Shrewsbury House, owned by the Earl of Shrewsbury, was on the north slope; its location was adjacent to the present Shrewsbury House, and Shrewsbury Park occupies part of the grounds. Only Severndroog Castle survives from this period.

From the early 19th century a hamlet had begun to grow; it later became a village, and can still readily be detected - around the church and the school, and on the opposite side of the road in Red Lion Lane (which was the original road to Woolwich), around the Red Lion, and in adjoining parts of the main road.

Growth of housing

By the late 19th century a number of large houses had been built in the woods to the south - these included Castle House, Castlewood House, Jackwood House, Wood Lodge, Summer Court, Warren Wood (where the writer Enid Bagnold lived 1903-20) and Falconwood House. All have now gone, though some lodges remain; their grounds now form the major part of the Shooters Hill Woods. Of several smaller villas which were built nearby on the main road during the same period, only Holbrook House and Derby Villas survive.

On the northern slopes from the 1860s a number of houses, some with very ornate features, appeared in streets nearer Plumstead and Woolwich. From the 1870s this development continued up Eglinton Hill and along Shrewsbury Lane, an older lane which linked Shooters Hill with Plumstead Common.

Apart from Red Lion Lane and Shrewsbury Lane, the area to the north of the main road was not developed for housing until the interwar period, and then only on the western side; as one descends eastwards from the summit, there is a large area of open space, comprising Eaglesfield Park and Shrewsbury Park, and the much larger Shooters Hill Golf Course and Woodlands Farm.

Woodlands Farm

The projected restoration of Woodlands Farm into an organic 'community' farm is a remarkable enterprise. It was a Co-op owned farm until the late 1980s. The Woodlands Farm Trust was set up to carry out the work in 1997, so the Farm is still in its early days, but it is already worth a visit. Public access is encouraged, and there are wonderful views over the rolling fields.

Shooters Hill Woods

The slopes to the south of Shooters Hill Road form an uninterrupted belt of woodland, comprising Eltham Common, Castle Wood, Jackwood and Oxleas Wood; and Shepherdleas Wood, in Eltham, is really a continuation of Oxleas Wood across Rochester Way. Much of these woodlands has been designated as a Site of Special Scientific Interest. They were purchased for the public by the London County Council between 1922 and 1938, and are now managed by the London Borough of Greenwich.

Large areas of the woods, particularly in Oxleas Wood, are classified as ancient woodland, ie. woodland where broad-leaved trees were not felled between c1600 and recent times. There is however a large variety of planted trees, remaining from the grounds of demolished mansions. The dominant large tree is the oak (some over 200 years old), and there are examples of sweet chestnut, beech, hornbeam, birch, pine, wild cherry, alder and ash, as well as the rarer wild service tree. Sections of the woodlands are coppiced, ie. cut down regularly, no longer for timber (as was the case until the 1920s) but in order to encourage small trees and shrubs, and there are extensive clumps of hazel, hawthorn, rhododendron, dogwood, elder, willow, rose, fern, holly etc. There are numerous types of fungi; and the insect life includes species of beetles, bugs, spiders and flies which are rare in Britain.

Fine views

As one would expect, there are fine views from many points in the area, and from several places one can on a clear day distinguish many landmarks of Central London.

The best views are from the top of Severndroog Castle, but it may not be easy to obtain access. Other good views are: towards Central London, from the top of Occupation Lane, from the small roundabouts in Moordown, and from the main road by the Samuel Phillips seat; to the north, from Shrewsbury Park; to the east, from Eaglesfield Park; and to the south, from the terrace in Castle Wood and from the cafe in Oxleas Wood.

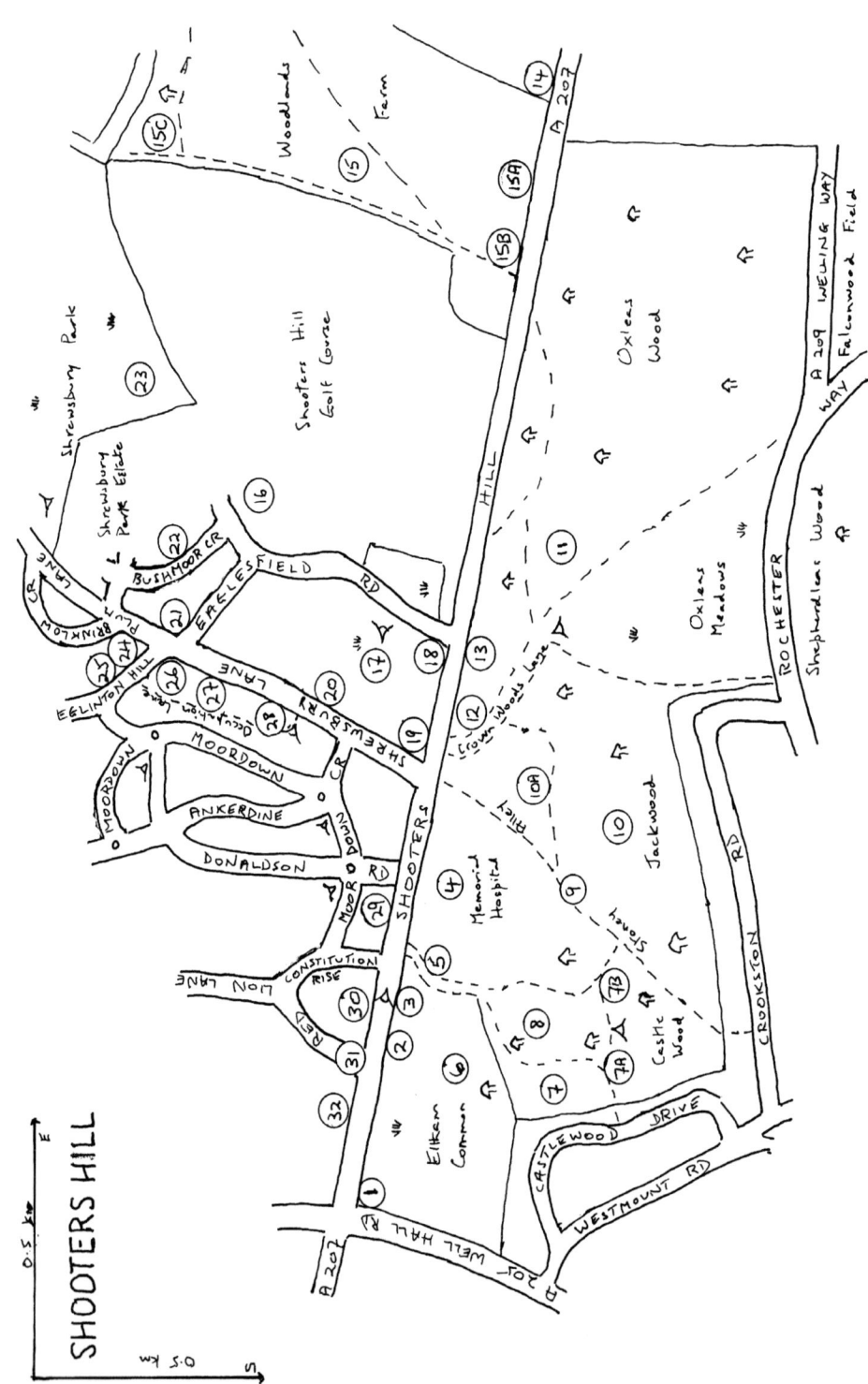

SHOOTERS HILL

Gazetteer

1. Shooters Hill Police Station. A red brick building of 1915 with a prominent full-height semi-circular bow window overlooking the road junction. Alongside in Shooters Hill is the **Old Police Station**, a classical building of 1852 in yellow brick. They form an interesting pair.

2. Christ Church. A small Victorian Gothic church of 1856, the east end added in 1869. The exterior is unexceptional, but the **interior** *(contact 1 Craigholm, Shooters Hill, or phone 020-8856 5858)* is interesting, with the atmosphere of a village church. Note the fine east end stained glass window of 1869 and a series of unusual roofshields. In 1900 Temple Moore added a coloured chancel screen, two large figures of winged angels in the chancel, and the decorated cornices.

In the churchyard is a graceful Great War memorial cross of granite, and in front of this is the **Ypres milestone** - an 18th century milestone converted to a first world war memorial. It reads: '130 miles to Ypres, in defending the salient our casualties were 90,000 killed, 70,500 missing, and 410,000 wounded'. Note the modern **milestone** on the opposite side of the road, with replicas of 19th century iron plates reading '8 miles to London Bridge' and '7 miles to Dartford', which used to be on the Ypres milestone.

To the east is **Christ Church School**. The small central building is the old village school of 1857; the extensions on either side are postwar.

3. The Samuel Phillips seat. This memorial seat of 1893 has a nice lych-gate style roof. There was originally a drinking fountain, but only the pipe remains. Samuel Phillips (who lived at Castle House - *see 5*) was a founder of the firm Johnson & Phillips, manufacturers of submarine cables, which was in Victoria Way, Charlton. The inscription reads 'Write me as one who loves his fellow men' (which is also on his tomb in Charlton Cemetery). From the main road at this point there is a fine **view** towards Central London.

4. Memorial Hospital, originally called the Woolwich & District War Memorial Hospital, later the Woolwich Memorial Hospital. A modest classical building of 1927, set in large grounds which include woodland similar to the adjoining Castle Wood. It was opened in memory of those killed in the first world war.

Just beyond the vestibule is the **Hall of Remembrance**, a small marble rotunda; note the enamelled roundel of The Good Samaritan by Gilbert Bayes, and stained glass windows of St Joan and St George.

5. Castle House Lodge. An early 19th century house, originally the lodge for Castle House (built 1823, demolished 1948), whose site is now in the grounds of the Memorial Hospital.

6. Eltham Common. An area of open space, which links Woolwich Common (of which it used to form part) with the Shooters Hill Woods. It is partly grassed and partly wooded, this part sharing the characteristics of the adjoining Castle Wood. It was purchased from the Army by the London County Council in 1938.

7. *Castle Wood. *(See Introduction, page 79.)* An area of woodland, in part forming a dense pattern of tall trees. Its dominant feature is Severndroog Castle *(see 8)*. Beyond is a large **rose garden (7A)**, which is on the site of Castlewood House (built 1870, demolished in the 1920s). The house and its grounds, including Severndroog Castle, were acquired by the London County Council in 1922.

Looking incongruous in the rose garden is a giant redwood tree. From the terrace above the garden there is a fine view southwards over Eltham towards the North Downs. To the east of the terrace is **Rose Cottage (7B)**, a highly ornamented house with rustic porch and great Dutch gables, probably of the 1870s, formerly the lodge for Castlewood House.

On the western edge of the Wood is a grassed area which covers a reservoir of 1920 *(see 18)*.

Access to the Wood (and to Severndroog Castle) is by a driveway between the Samuel Phillips seat and Craigholm, which leads to a car park and footpaths onwards. There is another access footpath from Castlewood Drive to the south. There is a network of footpaths through the Wood.

8. **Severndroog Castle. A tall triangular battlemented tower with hexagonal angle turrets, surrounded by the trees of Castle Wood; an extraordinary Gothic folly, it was built to a design of Richard Jupp in 1784. The original main entrance is on the south-west face; other original entrance doors are blocked, with only the fanlights remaining; the smaller doors under the turrets were added later. Note the quatrefoil windows at the top of each turret, otherwise all windows are pointed Gothic.

The inscription on the stone plaque over the original main entrance on the south-west face is transcribed on a tablet in a more legible position on the side facing north.

> Severndroog Castle was built by the widow of Sir William James, a commander in the East India Company, to celebrate his naval exploits, in particular his capture in 1755 of the island fortress of Severndroog (no longer existing) off the Malabar Coast of India. At that time the Castle was just north of the grounds of the James mansion of Park Farm Place, Eltham *(see Eltham 66)*. In 1870 the Castle became part of the grounds of Castlewood House, which was built on the wooded slopes below. The Castle and the House were sold to the London County Council in 1922.

From one of the turrets there are some of the finest **views** anywhere in London, unrestricted in all directions except to the north-east. The main room on the first floor has a fine ornamental plaster ceiling.

Severndroog Castle is not at present open to the public on any regular basis, but those with a special interest may be allowed access. Phone the Greenwich Rangers Service at Oxleas Wood on 020-8319 4253 for the latest information. The Castle is now on the market, and its future use is uncertain.

9. Stoney Alley. An old footpath running south from the main road, beginning just opposite the Bull pub and skirting the Memorial Hospital grounds. The southern part of the path forms the boundary between Castle Wood and Jackwood, and comes out in Crookston Road to the south. In the area near Rose Cottage are several very tall sweet chestnut trees.

10. *Jackwood. *(See Introduction, page 79.)* The north part of this large area of woodland, acquired by the London County Council in 1923, is dominated by the ornamental **terrace and gardens (10A)** of Jackwood House (built 1862, demolished in the 1920s) - note the fountain of 1873 with a lion's head. To the west of the terrace is an enclosed ornamental garden.

The site of the house is the area of flower-beds to the east of the terrace, and to the north of this site is a rather fanciful late 19th century house which was the staff quarters and stables. **The Lodge**, a house converted from two late 19th century cottages, one the lodge for Jackwood House, the other a gardener's cottage, is on Crown Woods Lane by the entrance into Jackwood.

Access to Jackwood is by Kenilworth Gardens and Crown Woods Lane, which leads to a car park. Jackwood is then accessed by taking the footpath alongside The Lodge on Crown Woods Lane. There is a network of footpaths through the Wood. Visitors are recommended to follow the signposts and markers for the Green Chain Walk.

11. *Oxleas Wood. *(See Introduction, page 79.)* A large wooded area, an outstanding example of surviving ancient woodland; it is amongst the oldest tracts of woodland in the London area. The woods are dense in places but interspersed with forest glades.

Oxleas Wood was acquired by the London County Council in 1934. Beforehand, much of the woods formed part of the grounds of Falconwood House (built 1867, demolished 1958), and this is the reason for the glades and, in the south-east corner of the woods, a stone-lined drinking pool for pheasants. (The driveway, now only a footpath, to Falconwood House still remains off the main road on the eastern slope, and the site of the House can be clearly identified at the end.)

Access to Oxleas Wood is by Kenilworth Gardens and Crown Woods Lane, which leads to a car park and a cafe. Straight ahead is Oxleas Meadows, and to the left Oxleas Wood. There are also footpaths into the Wood from further down the main road, and from Rochester Way and Welling Way to the south. There is a network of footpaths through the Wood. Visitors are recommended to follow the signposts and markers for the Green Chain Walk.

From the cafe near the entrance from Crown Woods Lane there are excellent views over **Oxleas Meadows** (which covers a large reservoir of 1983), and eastwards over Sidcup with the North Downs in the distance. The cafe is on the site of Wood Lodge (built c1780, demolished in the 1930s).

The woodland extends across Welling Way to the copse in **Falconwood Field**, and across Rochester Way to **Shepherdleas Wood** *(see Eltham 67B)*. These areas were cut off from Oxleas Wood when the roads were constructed in the early 1930s.

12. Holbrook House, 162 Shooters Hill. A stuccoed villa c1838, which may incorporate some late 18th century structure; the bay window was added in 1862, and extensions to the rear in the late 19th century.

13. Derby Villas, 176 Shooters Hill, a multi-gabled, very Gothic building of 1861.

14. We Anchor in Hope, 310 Bellegrove Road. An attractive brick pub of the 1850s, with a steeply pitched roof, looking more like a villa in its somewhat isolated location.

15. *Woodlands Farm, 331 Shooters Hill, is a 'community' farm, covering a large area, owned by the Woodlands Farm Trust, and operated with social and educational objectives. Since its purchase from the Co-op in 1997, the Trust has set out to create a working arable and livestock farm, on organic lines, providing an educational resource, and accessible to the public. A visit is strongly recommended, though it is unlikely to become fully operational as a farm until 2002. The rural landscape, consisting predominantly of a few large fields, offers wonderful open vistas, and so is complementary to the Shooters Hill Woods on the other side of the main road.

> Woodlands Farm has been farmland only since the early 19th century. In 1920 it was acquired by the Royal Arsenal Co-operative Society, and was until the late 1980s a working farm, one of very few surviving in Inner London. It was basically a pig farm, with its own abattoir. The Woodlands Farm Trust was formed in 1995 to save the farm and involve the local community; in 1997 the Trust purchased the farm from the Co-operative Wholesale Society, which had absorbed the RACS in 1985.

There are two houses on the main road. The larger house, called **Woodlands (15A)**, is a large and attractive house of 1886, with tiled upper floor and gables; the farm surrounds it, but it is not part of the farm. The smaller house to the west is in a similar style, c1894; it was the **farmhouse (15B)** until the farm closed, and is now the office of the Trust. Note the attractive garden in front of the house.

The farm is open 0930 to 1630 daily. Phone 020-8319 8900. The suggested walk of about three kilometres, described below, is only a brief summary. A leaflet describing in more detail this and other walks through the farm is available at the farmhouse.

Access to the farm is best through the gate adjoining the farmhouse. On the right is a old barn, planned as an Education Centre and already in use for educational purposes. To the left are two former piggeries, of the 1950s. Proceed north to the Woodlands Pond, then follow the path straight ahead alongside the golf course; there are magnificent rural views to the east over rolling fields. After some distance, turn sharp right to an area of concrete and rubble, which was the former Co-op abattoir site; on the other side of the path is **Clothworkers Wood (15C)**, a small area of ancient woodland. The path then leads past some allotments and along the perimeter of the farm; in due course, to the left there is access over a stream to the Green Chain Walk, which leads back to the main road, but keep to the path to the right, which leads westwards back to the pond and the farmhouse.

16. Lowood, Eaglesfield Road. A large house in stuccoed concrete of 1874; since 1925 it has been the clubhouse of the Shooters Hill Golf Club. The location of the house, with its wooded backcloth and the course sloping away, is magnificent. The east front, with its three distinctive gables, looks dramatic over the broad expanse of the golf course as one ascends the main road from the east.

17. Eaglesfield Park. This area of open space, on both sides of Eaglesfield Road, embraces the actual summit of the hill. There are sensational views towards the east over Erith, Bexleyheath and Bexley. Acquired by the London County Council 1908.

18. *Water Tower. A heavy fortress-like tower, octagonal and multi-coloured, of 1910, a prominent landmark which pinpoints Shooters Hill from afar. The detailing is extraordinary - note the triangular dormers, and on each face three round arches, below which are corbelling and elongated round-arched recesses with lancets. It was built to bring water to residents at the top of the hill; the water is forced up to the tower from a reservoir under Castle Wood *(see 7)* by a pumping station next to the Welcome Inn, Well Hall Road.

19. The Bull, a red brick pub of 1881, with good brick and terracotta work, and nicely curved bay windows. The date stone ('built 1749, rebuilt 1881') is over the original corner entrance, now bricked up. Note the sunflower motif on a bay to the left, and on the keystones above the upper floor windows. Just outside the door into the rear garden is a massive stone block, probably c1750.

About 65 metres to the east is **a horse mounting block** with three steps, dating back at least to 1750. It is in front of the site of the original pub called The Bull, which was a large and well-known tavern, built c1749 (possibly much earlier) and demolished in 1881. The block was re-erected here in 1929, but almost certainly the wrong way up.

Behind, and on part of the site of The Bull, is **157/9 Shooters Hill**, an amazing multi-gabled pair of 1907 with all sorts of ornamental flourishes, including blue brick diaper patterns and fantastic chimneys.

20. 40 Shrewsbury Lane, formerly known as Elmhurst Cottage. A weather-boarded cottage, rebuilt in 1975 as a replica of the original cottage of c1845.

21. Former Shooters Hill Fire Station, Eaglesfield Road. A handsome building of 1912 in Arts & Crafts style. Note the oriel windows, and the impressive skyline with closely packed dormers in the top storey (built as flats for firemen). The fire station closed in 1999, and the future use of the building is still uncertain.

22. Shrewsbury House, Bushmoor Crescent. A large building of 1923 in classical style; note the large front portico of Ionic columns, the ground floor bow windows facing north, and to the rear a curved loggia also with Ionic columns. It is located adjacent to the site of an older house with the same name (built 1789 for the Earl of Shrewsbury, leased in 1799 to the Crown for the young Princess Charlotte, daughter of the Prince Regent, demolished 1923). It is now in use as a community centre.

It is situated on the **Shrewsbury Park Estate**, an attractively laid out 'garden suburb' style estate with several greens, built in the grounds of Shrewsbury House in the 1930s.

23. Shrewsbury Park. An extensive park with a wooded area and wildlife sanctuary, its lower slopes giving excellent views over Plumstead, Thamesmead and the Thames. It was once part of the grounds of Shrewsbury House, which were purchased by the London County Council in 1928.

24. A round barrow, possibly dating back to the Bronze Age, at the junction of Brinklow Crescent and Plum Lane. This burial mound is the sole survivor of several on Shooters Hill, the others having been destroyed in building works in the 1930s.

25. 133/155 Eglinton Hill form an imposing group going downhill on the east side of the road. All houses have projecting bay windows through two storeys. Nos 133/143 are probably of the 1870s. Nos 145/7, of c1898, has attractive ornamental features, including a head within a medallion in the pedimented gable-end. Nos 149/51 are c1899, and nos 153/5 c1902.

26. 100 Eglinton Hill, formerly known as Cheviot Lodge. A large and rather eccentric house c1868, with a large extension of 1882. It is difficult to identify the original house because of extensions and conservatories. Riverview Heights, a long block of flats, was built in the grounds in the 1950s.

27. 91 Shrewsbury Lane, a small stuccoed Regency-style house, probably of the 1870s, with an elegant iron balcony.

28. Occupation Lane. This lane, almost rural in parts, winds round the back of Shrewsbury Lane to join Eglinton Hill; it was laid out as a mews in the late 19th century, and has modern houses as well as old cottages. At the top it is flanked to the left by a stretch of 18th century walling (there is another stretch of 18th century walling between 59 & 61 Shrewsbury Lane), and there is a magnificent view westwards towards Central London.

29. The raised pavement at this point on Shooters Hill, opposite the Memorial Hospital, indicates the original level and contour of the Dover Road before the gradients were eased by the New Cross Turnpike Trust c1817.

Another section of raised pavement can be seen nearby on the east side of Shrewsbury Lane.

30. The Red Lion. A pub of 1902, replacing a much older building located slightly to the north. It is attractive externally and internally. Note the grotesque figure on top of the sharp corner gable. The pub is at the centre of **Red Lion Place**, an interesting enclave; the houses to the right are of 1886 and the houses to the left of 1902.

Adjacent but on the main road to the east are **53/57 Shooters Hill**, an interesting group. No 53 is a house c1835 with a modern shopfront, no 55 is of 1886, and no 57 (Prospect Cottage) is basically late 18th century, though its present facade with striking Gothick windows is probably c1816.

31. Red Lion Lane. This was the original road from Shooters Hill to Woolwich. The southern part is a tree-lined slightly winding village-type street, with considerable atmosphere. The west side consists mainly of long terraces of older houses. Note in particular: nos 128/144, c1902, with nice decorative details; no 126, of the 1840s, an attractive detached house with distinctive features; nos 98/102 (Elizabeth Cottages) and nos 50/68, both mid 19th century. The other terraces are late 19th century.

32. Signpost Castlewood Centre, originally Woolwich & Plumstead Cottage Hospital, and still in Health Service use. An unusual vernacular building of 1889, with a tile-hung upper floor and attractive decorative features. Note the foundation stone by the entrance.

SHOOTERS HILL

Suggested Walk

It is recommended that the suggested walk be followed in conjunction with the Gazetteer and the map, and that the Gazetteer be consulted at each location. Most locations described in the Gazetteer are covered; some locations have not been included, as they might add too much to the length of the walk. In particular, Woodlands Farm needs a special visit.

The walk begins and ends at the Police Station at the bottom of the west slope of Shooters Hill. It follows a more or less circular route, so can be joined at any point. Distance approx four kilometres. The walk will be appreciated best if taken on a clear day, because of the many fine views. There is quite a steep ascent up the main road at the beginning of the walk.

The walk can of course be extended by walks through the woodlands, though this may add considerably to the distance covered. Bear in mind that the footpaths can become very muddy at times.

NB. It is worth trying to make advance arrangements - see the Gazetteer - to view the interior of Christ Church.

From the **Police Station (1)**, proceed up Shooters Hill on the south side of the road, with **Eltham Common (6)** on the right. On reaching **Christ Church (2)**, try to see the interior, and note the war memorial and the **Ypres milestone** in front. Continue up the hill to the **Samuel Phillips seat (3)**; look back for the view towards Central London at this point, then take the access road immediately to the right. Pass **Castle House Lodge (5)** on the left, and enter **Castle Wood (7)**. Proceed ahead on the footpath to **Severndroog Castle (8)** and beyond, descending the steps to the **rose garden (7A)**. Return up the steps to the first terrace and turn right along the path to **Rose Cottage (7B)**.

Continue to the footpath ahead, which is **Stoney Alley (9)**. Follow the Green Chain Walk markers into **Jackwood (10)** until you come to the ornamental **terrace and gardens (10A)**. Continue past the gardens and take the footpath to the left until you come to **The Lodge**. Turn right into Crown Woods Lane and enter **Oxleas Wood (11)**. Continue to the cafe for the view, then retrace steps along Crown Woods Lane, passing The Lodge, until you come out to the main road. Note **Holbrook House (12)** on the right.

Cross the road to **The Bull (19)**, with the **mounting block** and **157/9 Shooters Hill** to the right. Bear right past the **Water Tower (18)**, noting **Derby Villas (13)** opposite. Turn left into Eaglesfield Road, walk up into **Eaglesfield Park (17)** for the view to the east, then continue along Eaglesfield Road as it bears left to the crossroads, noting the former **Shooters Hill Fire Station (21)** on the right.

Bear right and cross to the **round barrow (24)** on the corner of Plum Lane and Brinklow Crescent. Walk along Plum Lane, then turn right into Mereworth Drive, and right again into Bushmoor Crescent, and continue to **Shrewsbury House (22)**. Retrace steps to the round barrow, then turn right down **Eglinton Hill**. Note **nos 133/155 (25)** on the right, then retrace steps to the top, noting **no 100 (26)** at the junction.

Turn right along **Shrewsbury Lane**, passing **no 91 (27)**, until you reach the top of **Occupation Lane (28)** and its view. Continue along Shrewsbury Lane, noting **no 40 (20)** on the left, then turn right down Ankerdine Crescent to the roundabout, with its fine view, turn left along Moordown, and left again into Donaldson Road, then right onto Shooters Hill.

Walk along the **raised pavement (29)**, noting the **Memorial Hospital (4)** opposite, and descend the hill. Note on the right **53/57 Shooters Hill**, and **The Red Lion (30)** in the enclave of **Red Lion Place**, then turn right into **Red Lion Lane (31)**. Walk a short way down, at least to no 126, and retrace steps. Continue down the hill, passing **Signpost Castlewood Centre (32)**, until you return to the Police Station.

Notes on some Architects & Artists

NB. The gazetteer references are as follows: E = Eltham, NE = New Eltham, M = Mottingham, K = Kidbrooke, SH = Shooters Hill.

Maurice Adams, 1849-1933 *(E 32)*. A prolific architect of the Edwardian Baroque; he designed Eltham Library and the School of Art, Art Gallery and Baths at Camberwell.

Thomas Aldwinckle, 1844-1930 *(K 16)*. An architect of South East London, he designed the former Brook Hospital, Kentish Town Public Baths, and the Public Baths and Louise House at Forest Hill.

John Bacon the Younger, 1777-1859 *(E 20)*. Classical sculptor, and son of the more famous John Bacon. His work included the William III statue in St James Square; Father Thames at Ham House and at Terrace Gardens, Richmond; and several memorials in St Pauls Cathedral.

Thomas Bailey *(E 60, NE 4)*. Architect to the London School Board from 1884 to 1910. He developed the style of his predecessor Edward Robson into more classical forms.

Sir Frank Baines *(E 72)*. As principal architect of the Office of Works, he was responsible for building several estates for munitions workers in the first world war; the most remarkable was the Well Hall Estate (later Progress Estate) at Eltham.

Gilbert Bayes, 1872-1953 *(SH 4)*. Sculptor of the statue of Joseph Priestley in Russell Square, and 'Play up, Play up!' on the wall of Lords Cricket Ground.

John Belcher, 1841-1913 *(K 6)*. A leading architect of the Edwardian Baroque style, particularly in association with John James Joass. His most important buildings were the Institute of Chartered Accountants and Colchester Town Hall.

Alfred Blomfield, 1879-1949 *(E 64)*. Chief architect of the South Eastern and Chatham Railway, and then of Watneys, for whom he designed numerous pubs in the London area. No relation of

Sir Arthur Blomfield, 1829-99 *(E 20, 39)*. An architect of the Victorian Gothic revival. His works included the Royal College of Music and Selwyn College, Cambridge, as well as numerous churches. The firm of Sir Arthur Blomfield & Son continued to do important work after his death.

Sir Reginald Blomfield, 1856-1942 *(K 6)*. Nephew of Sir Arthur Blomfield. From 1895 he became an advocate of Edwardian neo-classicism. He designed the Regent Street quadrant and the western part of Piccadilly Circus.

Burlison & Grylls, founded 1868 *(E 20)*, a firm whose stained glass, mainly of the Gothic revival, can be seen in numerous churches throughout the country.

Nugent Francis Cachemaille-Day, 1896-1976 *(E 7)*. A pioneer of modern church architecture in the 1930s. His most famous churches are St Saviours Eltham and St Nicholas, Burnage, Manchester.

90 - NOTES ON SOME ARCHITECTS & ARTISTS

William Douglas Caroë, 1857-1938 *(E 39)*. Architect to the Ecclesiastical Commissioners, and a prolific church architect, restorer and designer. He designed the Archbishop's Palace at Canterbury.

Sir Ninian Comper, 1864-1960 *(E 20)*. He specialised in church monuments, and also restored and designed many churches.

Ralph Covell, d1988 *(M 18A)*. A modern church architect with a highly individual style. His local churches include St Laurence Catford, St Alban Mottingham, and William Temple at Abbey Wood. He also designed the Piccadilly Hotel, Manchester.

Edward Cullinan *(E 59C)*. A highly regarded contemporary architect with an eclectic and idiosyncratic style. Architect of a number of striking buildings for Olivetti. In the London area, he has designed a number of small-scale housing schemes, and was responsible for the rebuilding of Barnes Church.

Thomas Cutler, 1842-1909 *(E 52)*. His most famous work was the mansion and other buildings at Avery Hill. He also designed the Hotel Metropole, Folkestone.

Samuel Dottridge *(K 8, 14)*, an architect of Blackheath, who lived in Liskeard Gardens.

Hans Feibusch *(E 71)*. German-born mural painter who settled in London in the 1930s. He has done murals in many postwar church buildings and church restorations in South London.

Thomas Ford *(E 20, 71; NE 9; K 5)*. An architectural practice which has since the war built many churches and carried out many restorations, often with rather startling interiors, in South London.

Alfred Hardiman, 1891-1949 *(E 1)*. Sculptor of the Haig statue in Whitehall; 'Peace' and a fountain in St James Churchyard, Piccadilly; and St George at Eltham Palace.

John Hayward *(E 7)*. Designer of stained glass and other furnishings in many postwar churches and restorations in London.

O'Hanlon Hughes *(E 74)*. Architect of Roman Catholic churches in the 1930s. He designed St Edmunds at Beckenham and The Martyrs at Eltham.

George Hubbard, 1859-1936 *(M 4, 16)*. An architect of Mottingham, who lived in a (now demolished) house in West Park. He designed Geffery's Court & the War Memorial, as well as Witanhurst, Highgate West Hill, and houses in Wimbledon.

John James Joass, 1868-1952 *(K 6)*. An architect in the Edwardian Baroque style, who worked in association with John Belcher and became the dominant influence in the partnership from 1906. He designed the Mappin Terraces at London Zoo.

Richard Jupp, d1799 *(SH 8)*. Surveyor to the East India Company. He built Guys Hospital, the Manor House at Lee, and Severndroog Castle.

C. E. Kempe, founded 1869 *(E 39)*, a firm whose stained glass, mainly of the Gothic revival, can be seen in numerous churches throughout the country.

Gilbert Ledward, 1888-1960 *(E 1)*. Professor of Sculpture at the Royal College of Art. His main works are the Guards Memorial at Horse Guards Parade, and the Venus fountain in Sloane Square. A series of his sculptures is in the grounds of the Stoke-on-Trent City Museum.

Sir Peter Lely, 1618-80 *(E 16)*. Leading portrait painter, of Dutch origin, whose studio was closely associated with the court of Charles II.

Peter Malacrida, c1889-c1980 *(E 1)*. In the practice of White Allom, he was a leading interior designer in London in the interwar period, specialising in the style of the Florentine renaissance.

Andrew Mather, 1891-1938 *(E 49, 70)*. Leading cinema architect, especially of Odeon cinemas, including the one in Leicester Square.

Hugh May, 1622-84 *(E 16)*. A precursor of Wren, he was a pioneer of the classical revival. Eltham Lodge, his sole surviving London building, was the first domestic building in the new classical style.

Temple Moore, 1856-1920 *(E 61; SH 2)*. A prolific builder, restorer and decorator of churches.

Lord Mottistone, the former John Seely, 1899-1963 *(E 1)*. With Paul Paget, 1901-85, the partnership carried out much rebuilding, restoration and design of new furnishings in London churches before and after the last war. Their work is in St Pauls Cathedral, Westminster Abbey and Lambeth Palace. Their principal secular building was Eltham Hall (now Courtauld House).

Philip Robson, 1871-1951 *(K 13)*. Son of the London School Board architect Edward Robson. He designed St Gabriels College Camberwell, St Andrews Church Catford, and the Eastbourne Library & Technical Institute.

Sir George Gilbert Scott, 1811-78 *(E 71)*. One of the most prolific architects in and propagandists for the Victorian Gothic style. His work, a major contribution to the London scene, included St Pancras Station, the Albert Memorial, and the Foreign Office (where Lord Palmerston insisted on a classical style). His numerous churches included St Mary Abbots at Kensington and St Giles at Camberwell, and he was a major restorer at Westminster Abbey.

Sir Giles Gilbert Scott, 1880-1960 *(E 6)*. Grandson of Sir George Gilbert Scott. Architect of Liverpool Anglican Cathedral, Battersea Power Station and Waterloo Bridge; and designer of the old red cast-iron telephone kiosks.

Michael Searles, 1750-1813 *(K10A)*. A Georgian architect of South-East London, with a particularly elegant style. In addition to individual houses, he was the designer of several architectural compositions like The Paragon at Blackheath and Gloucester Circus at Greenwich.

George Street, 1824-81 *(E 39)* A leading Victorian Gothic architect, whose greatest work, the Royal Courts of Justice, represents the triumph of the style.

John Whichcord, 1823-85 *(K 11A)*. A prominent architect of the later 19th century, specialising in commercial buildings in Central London. His most famous work is the Grand Hotel at Brighton.

BIBLIOGRAPHY

(including books and publications consulted, and books recommended for further reading, especially for information on local history and architectural detail.)

London 2: South, by Bridget Cherry & Nikolaus Pevsner (Buildings of England series, Penguin Books, 1983)
Handbook to the Environs of London, by James Thorne (1876, republished 1970)
The Story of Royal Eltham, by R. R. C. Gregory (1909)
Eltham Palace, by Michael Turner (English Heritage 1999)
Eltham Palace, by D. E. Strong (Department of the Environment 1958, republished by English Heritage 1986)
The Story of Eltham Palace, by Roy Brook (1960)
Nature Conservation in Greenwich (London Ecology Unit 1989)
Green Chain Walk, leaflets nos 1 / 4
The Industrial Archaeology of South East London (Goldsmiths College Industrial Archaeology Group 1982)
Lewisham to Dartford via Bexleyheath and Sidcup, by Vic Mitchell & Keith Smith (London Suburban Railways, Middleton Press 1991)
The Bexleyheath Line, by Dr Edwin Course (Oakwood Press)
The Dartford Loop Line, by R. W. Kidner (Oakwood Press, 1966)
The Bexleyheath Railway at Eltham, by Gus White (Eltham Society 1996)
Looking at Eltham (Eltham Society 1970)
Looking into Eltham (Eltham Society 1980)
Eltham in the Making, Volume 1 (Eltham Society 1990)
Some Eltham Local History Records (Eltham Society 1977)
People around a Palace, by Sally Simmons & Margaret Taylor (1991)
Severndroog Castle & Sir William James (Eltham Society 1984)
The Tarn, by Jane Chandley & Margaret Taylor (Eltham Society 1987)
Eltham, a Pictorial History, by John Kennett (1995)
Thomas Philipot's Almshouse Charity, by John Kennett (1997)
The Eltham Hutments, by John Kennett (1985)
Teachers in Training 1906-1985, A History of Avery Hill College, by David Shorney (Thames Polytechnic 1989)
An Illustrated History of the University of Greenwich, by Thomas Hinde (University of Greenwich 1996)
Looking back at Eltham, by Ron Roffey (CWS South East Co-op, 1993)
Churches in the Hundred of Blackheath, by L. A. J. Baker (Greenwich & Lewisham Antiquarian Society 1961)
A Walk around Eltham Parish Church, by Margaret Taylor (1986)
Parish Churches of London, by Basil Clarke (Batsford, 1966)
Catholic Churches of London, by Dennis Evinson (Sheffield Academic Press, 1998)
In memory of Yemmerawanyea, by Margaret Taylor (St Johns Church 1994)
Holy Trinity Church Eltham, a brief history & guide, by Pat Caffarey & Anthea Gent

BIBLIOGRAPHY - 93

Well Hall, by F. C. Elliston-Erwood (Metropolitan Borough of Woolwich 1947)
A Tudor Building at Well Hall, by Reg Rigden (London Borough of Greenwich 1970, later revised)
Well Hall, archaeological appraisal by The Conservation Practice, for English Heritage (1994)
A Woman of Passion, the life of E Nesbit, by Julia Briggs (1987)
E. Nesbit in Eltham, by Margaret Taylor (Eltham Society 1974, revised 1999)
A Walk in New Eltham (Eltham Society 1980, revised 1993)
A History of the Church and Parish of All Saints New Eltham, by Rev Michael Kingston (1979, revised 1998)
Mottingham, from hamlet to urban village, by Wynn Parkinson (Bromley Libraries 1977)
Centenary, the story of the first 100 years in the life of St Andrew Mottingham, by Elizabeth Horsman (1979)
Walk around Mottingham Village, by Ian Murdock (1981)
The parish & church of St Edward the Confessor Mottingham, by Ian Murdock (1983)
Blackheath Village & Environs - Volume 2, by Neil Rhind (1983)
Kidbrooke, by Michael Egan (Greenwich & Lewisham Antiquarian Society 1983)
St James Kidbrooke, by Ursula Mason (1967)
The Quaggy River and its Catchment Area, by Ken White (1999)
Aspects of Shooters Hill (Shooters Hill Local History Group, No 1 1984 & No 2 1989)
Articles on Shooters Hill, by Col A. H. Bagnold, from Christ Church Parish Magazine (1936-38)
Old Ordnance Survey maps, published by Alan Godfrey - Eltham 1894, Mottingham 1861, Mottingham 1894, Kidbrooke 1894, Shooters Hill 1866, Shooters Hill 1914
The Newsletters of *The Eltham Society*
Various articles in Proceedings of the *Woolwich & District Antiquarian Society*
Various articles in Transactions of the *Greenwich & Lewisham Antiquarian Society (now Greenwich Historical Society)*

All the above publications, and of course many more books, maps and documents, can be consulted at **Greenwich Local History Library**, Woodlands, Mycenae Road, London SE3 (phone 020-8858 4631). Documents etc on Mottingham can be consulted at **Bromley Local Studies Centre**, Central Library, High Street, Bromley (phone 020-8460 9955).

INDEX

(Gazetteer references - E = Eltham, NE = New Eltham, M = Mottingham, K = Kidbrooke, SH = Shooters Hill)

Architects & Artists
  Maurice Adams - E 32
  Robert Adams - E 8
  Thomas Aldwinckle - K 16
  Leopoldo Ansiglioni - E 52C
  Carlton Attwood - E 1
  John Bacon the Younger - E 20
  Thomas Bailey - E 60; NE 4
  Sir Frank Baines - E 72
  B. E. Barber - E 20
  Gilbert Bayes - SH 4
  John Belcher - K 6
  Caroline Benyon - NE 9
  Alfred Blomfield - E 64
  Sir Arthur Blomfield - E 20, 39
  Sir Reginald Blomfield - K 6
  Stan Boundy - E 71
  F. G. Broadbent & Partners - E 36
  Burlison & Grylls - E 20
  James Butler - E 36
  Nicholas Burwell - E 17A
  Nugent Cachemaille-Day - E 7
  Edward Clarke - M 2
  Lindsay Clarke - E 74
  W. D. Caroë - E 39
  Harry Clark - E 36
  Sir Ninian Comper - E 20
  Paul Cookson - E 24
  Ralph Covell - M 18A
  Margaret Cowell - E 39, 69C
  Edward Cullinan - E 59C
  Thomas Cutler - E 52
  Trevor Dannatt - E 50
  Samuel Dottridge - E 8, 14
  Thomas Norman Dinwiddy - K 6
  Peter Dollar - NE 9
  Marion Dorn - E 1
  Edwards & Powell - K 5
  Rolf Engströmer - E 1
  Hans Feibusch - E 71
  Thomas Ford - E 20, 71; NE 9; K 5
  Sir Douglas Galton - K 17
  Kruger Gray - E 1
  Alfred Hardiman - E 1
  Donald Hastings - E 7
  John Hayward - E 7
  Margaret Higginson - K 4
  O'Hanlon Hughes - E 74
  George Hubbard - M4, 16
  Charles Sargeant Jagger - E 1
  John James Joass - K 6

  Richard Jupp - SH 8
  C. E. Kempe - E 39
  Laurence King - E 7
  Gilbert Ledward - E 1
  Sir Peter Lely - E 16
  Filippo Locatelli - E 1
  F. E. McWilliam - E 52G
  Peter Malacrida - E 1
  Andrew Mather - E 49, 70
  Hugh May - E 16
  Temple Moore - E 61; SH 2
  Newman & Billing - K 5
  Paul Paget - E 1, 5A
  Philip Robson - K 13
  Scoles & Raymond - E 36
  Sir George Gilbert Scott - E 71
  Sir Giles Gilbert Scott - E 6
  Michael Searles - K 10A
  John Seely (Lord Mottistone) - E 1, 5A
  Carter Shapland - M 18A
  Slater, Uren & Pike - K 15
  Sir John Soane - E 1
  George Street - E 39
  Campbell Taylor - E 1
  Arthur Torrance - K 7
  Paul Velluet - E 39
  Jerk Werkmäster - E 1
  David Whalley - E 74
  John Whichcord - K 11A
  Whitefriars Studio - E 39

Churches
  All Saints - NE 9
  Blackheath & Charlton Baptist - K 14
  Christ Church Shooters Hill- SH 2
  Christ Church Eltham- E 36
  Eltham Park Baptist - E 65
  Eltham Park Chapel - E 62
  Eltham Park Methodist - E 63
  Eltham United Reformed - E 18
  Holy Trinity - E 39
  The Martyrs - E 74
  Mottingham Methodist - M 14
  Our Lady Help of Christians - M 15
  St Albans - M 18A
  St Andrews - M 2
  St Barnabas - E 71
  St Edward the Confessor - M 17A
  St James - K 5
  St John the Baptist - E 20
  St Luke - E 61
  St Saviour - E 7

INDEX - 95

Housing developments
  Arnold House - K 13
  Brook Estate - page 69
  Brook Mews - K 17
  Brook Village - K 16
  Cedar Mount - M 8C
  Clare Corner - NE 4
  Coldharbour Estate - M 18
  Colview Court - M 8A
  Daisy Munns House - NE 13
  Eltham Heights Estate - page 14
  Eltham Park Estate - E 59
  Evelyn Estate - page 69
  Ferrier Estate - K 2
  Fifteenpenny Fields - E 34
  Geffery's Court - M 16
  Horn Park Estate - E 11
  Lower Brook Estate - page 69
  Middle Park Estate - E 6
  Mottingham Estate - M 17
  Page Estate - page 14
  Philipot Almshouses - E 44A
  Progress Estate - E 72
  Royal Herbert Pavilions - K 17
  Shrewsbury Park Estate - SH 22
  Southend House - E 40
  Theobalds Cottages - NE 16
  Victoria Cottages - NE 6

Industrial archaeology
  The Arcade - E 29
  Cliftons Service Station - E 10
  Conduit head - E 38
  Eltham Park Station (remains) - E 64
  Eltham Station - E 58
  Falconwood Station - E 57
  Finger signposts - E 52G; NE 5
  Haworth Graves - M 13
  Horse troughs - E 9, 54; NE 5
  Ice-well - E 14
  Kidbrooke Station - K 1
  Letter-boxes - M 3, 8B; K 6, 16
  Milestones - E 40, 47, 51; NE 11;
  K 10; SH 2
  Mottingham Farm - M 4E
  Mottingham Station - M 1
  Mounting block - SH 19
  New Eltham Station - NE 1
  Raised pavement - SH 29
  Stanleys - NE 12
  Telephone kiosks - E 6
  Water towers - E 52; K 16; SH 18

Leisure
  Bob Hope Theatre - E 46
  Coronet Cinema (former)- E 70
  Mecca Bingo - E 49
  Winter Garden - E 52C

Parks, Woods and Open Spaces
  Avery Hill Park & fields - E 48E
  Castle Wood - SH 7
  Clothworkers Wood - SH 15C
  Conduit Meadow - E 38
  The Course - M 18
  Eaglesfield Park - SH 17
  Eltham Cemetery - E 56
  Eltham Common - SH 6
  Eltham Green - E 9
  Eltham Park - E 67
  Environmental Curric. Centre - E 53
  Greenwich Cemetery - K 18
  Harmony Wood - E 13
  Horn Park - E 11
  Jackwood - SH 10
  Kidbrooke Green - K 3
  King George's Field - K 18A
  King John's Walk fields - E 5
  Lovelace Green - E 72B
  Mottingham Farm fields - M 10
  Oxleas Wood - SH 11
  Pippenhall Meadows - E 51
  St Johns Burial Ground - E 20A
  Shepherdleas Wood - E 67B
  Shrewsbury Park - SH 23
  Southwood Rough - NE 8B
  The Tarn - E 14
  Well Hall Pleasaunce - E 69B
  Woodlands Farm - SH 15

People
  John Arnold - E 69
  Hubert Bland - E 69
  William Blenkiron - E 20A
  Geoffrey Chaucer - E 1
  Cameron Corbett - E 59
  Sir Stephen & Virginia Courtauld - E 1
  Thomas Doggett - E 20
  Ellen Thorneycroft Fowler - E 3B
  W. G. Grace - M 8H
  Bill Hamling MP - E 7
  Thomas Chester Haworth - M 13
  Bob Hope - E 46, 59B
  Frankie Howerd - E 21, 71
  Sir William James - E 20A, 66; SH 8
  King Jean le Bon - E 1
  Richard Jefferies - E 43
  Prince John of Eltham - E 1
  Stephen Lawrence - E 73
  Herbert Morrison - E 31
  Edith Nesbit - E 69
  John North - E 20A, 39, 52
  Nicholas Ogareff - K 18
  Kitty O'Shea - E 16
  Sir Gregory Page - E 69
  Samuel Phillips - SH 3
  William Roper - E 69

Sir John Shaw - E 16
Anne Wood - E 15, 16
Yemmerrawanyeah Kebbarah - E 20A
Public buildings (present and former)
   Brook Hospital - K 16
   Eltham Fire Station - E 35
   Eltham Library - E 32
   Eltham and Mottingham House - E 24
   Memorial Hospital - SH 4
   New Eltham Library - NE 7
   Royal Herbert Hospital - K 17
   St Marys Centre - E 30
   Shooters Hill Fire Station - SH 21
   Shooters Hill Police Station - SH 1
   Shrewsbury House - SH 22
   Signpost Castlewood Centre -SH 32
Pubs etc
   Bankers Draft - E 21
   Beehive - NE 3
   Bull - SH 19
   Chequers - E 47
   Dutch House - E 12
   Eletriq cafe - E 32
   Greyhound - E 22
   Mellins wine bar- E 23
   Old Post Office - E 24
   Park Tavern - E 24
   Porcupine - M 11B
   Red Lion - SH 30
   Rising Sun - E 32
   Sun in the Sands - K 10D
   Tudor Barn - E 69C
   We Anchor in Hope - SH 14
Schools and Colleges
   Avery Hill Campus - E 52
   Christ Church - SH 2
   Crown Woods - E 55
   Deansfield - E 68
   Eltham C of E - E 29
   Eltham College - M 7
   Eltham Green - E 8
   Eltham Hill - E 50
   Gordon - E 60
   Hadlow College Mottingham - M 9
   Kidbrooke - K 15
   St Marys - E 66
   Thomas Tallis - K 4
   Wyborne - NE 4
Streets and paths
   Archery Road - E 31
   Arsenal Road - E 72
   Avery Hill Road - E 52; NE 12-13, 16
   Balcaskie Road - E 59
   Beechhill Road - E 59
   Blanmerle Road - NE 2
   Blunts Road - E 34
   Cambridge Green - NE 5

Court Road - E 15, 16, 18; M 2, 3B
Court Yard - E 1, 2, 3, 19
Craigton Road - E 59, 59B
Devonshire Road - M 11C
Dunvegan Road - E 59
Eaglesfield Road - SH 15-16, 20
Earlshall Road - E 59
Eglinton Hill - SH 25-26
Elizabeth Terrace - E 45
Eltham High Street - E 20-23, 25-28, 30, 32-33, 35-36, 47, 59A
Eltham Hill - E 48-50
Eltham Park Gardens - E 59
Footscray Rd - E 40-43; NE 3-5, 10-11
Glenesk Road - E 59
Glenhouse Road - E 59
Glenlyon Road - E 59
Glenshiel Road - E 59
Glenure Road - E 66
Gourock Road - E 59
Gravel Pit Lane - E 54
Green Lane - NE 6
Greenholm Road - E 59, 59C
Greenvale Road - E 59
Grove Park Road - M 6-7
Hervey Road - K 12
Kidbrooke Gardens - K 7
Kidbrooke Grove - K 6
Kidbrooke Park Road - K 1-2, 4-5, 11
King John's Walk - E 5; M 8
Liskeard Gardens - K 8
Merchland Road - NE 14
Middle Park Avenue - E 6-7
Mottingham Lane - M 8-10
Mottingham Road - M 5, 11, 14-16
North Park - E 17
Occupation Lane - SH 28
Passey Place - E 24
Philipot Path - E 44
Phineas Pett Road - E 72
Prince Rupert Road - E 72
Red Lion Lane - SH 31
Roper Street - E 29
Ross Way - E 72
St Germans Place - K 9
Shooters Hill - SH 1-4, 12-13, 15, 18, 19, 29-32
Shooters Hill Rd - K 10, 13-14, 16-17
Shrewsbury Lane - SH 20-21, 27
Southend Crescent - E 37-39
Southwood Road - NE 8
Sparrows Lane - NE 15
Tilt Yard Approach - E 4
Well Hall Road - E 69-70, 72-74; K 18
West Park - M 3
Westmount Road - E 59, 61, 63-65, 67
Whinyates Road - E 72
Wythfield Road - E 46